Farm Journal's Everyday Favorite Recipes

Farm Journal's
Everyday
Favorite Recipes

By the Food Editors of Farm Journal

Farm Journal, Inc., Philadelphia, Pennsylvania

Book Design: Rick Gribbin
Cover Design: Rick Gribbin
Cover Photo: William Hazzard

Library of Congress Cataloging In Publication Data
Main entry under title: Farm journal's everyday favorite recipes
Includes index.
1. Cookery. I. Farm journal (Philadelphia, 1956-   )
II. Title: Everyday favorite recipes.
TX715.F2243   641.5   80-19769
ISBN: 0-89795-011-9

Contents

Introduction

We know that preparing everyday meals is a top problem with most homemakers. In a recent survey of the Farm Journal Family Test Group, many farm and ranch women told us that they needed more help with everyday meal planning. Today's busy homemakers—in city or country—just don't have the time to search through several cookbooks for dishes that appeal to their families and fit into hectic time schedules.

To make everyday meal planning easier, we've put 110 family favorites into just one cookbook, the one you now have in your hands. You can give everyday meals a lift when you add these country specials to your usual round of family dishes. Each recipe was selected to give variety to daily menus and stretch your food dollar without short-changing your family's nutritive needs.

To give you help in finding just the dish you need, we have divided this collection into four chapters: dinner entrées, luncheon specials, vegetable or salad side dishes and desserts.

Each and every recipe has been tested, tasted and approved in our famous Farm Journal Test Kitchens by staff home economists.

With these recipes at your fingertips, you'll be able to turn out appetizing dishes every day with confidence and ease.

Chapter One

Hearty Dinner Entrées

Selecting an appetizing main dish—one your family likes—is a decision you make every day. Because we know you're extra-busy, we've collected main dish recipes that can be served without a flurry of last-minute preparation. This chapter features 37 recipes—each is easy-on-the-budget, quickly prepared and made from ingredients found in most country kitchens.

Hearty but simply made entrées, such as Deviled Swiss Steak, a tender round steak with carrots and tomatoes, or Oven-Barbecued Chicken, with its homemade spicy sauce, are baked in the oven with little attention from you. Other oven favorites include five different meat loaves— each one distinctive and flavorful. For instance, our Ham and Pork Loaf is a delightful combination of ground ham, pork and rice seasoned with cloves and minced parsley and served with a delicately flavored

Mustard-Egg Sauce.

Busy women are always on the lookout for one-dish dinners, so we have selected 24 stews, casseroles and main dish pies. You'll find enticing new combinations and old favorites, some using leftovers and others starting from scratch. In Chicken-Ham Casserole, leftover chicken and ham are transformed into a complete meal-in-a-dish when combined with chicken broth, light cream, mushrooms, peas and spaghetti.

More and more farm wives are turning to their slow cookers during the extra-busy planting and harvesting seasons. You'll note that we have included four choices: Texican Chili, made with cubed beef; Rosemary Lamb Stew; Two-Step Bean Cassoulet and Herbed Chicken Cacciatore.

As you browse through this chapter, you'll find nourishing dinner recipes that insure good eating every day.

Deviled Swiss Steak

⅓ c. flour
1 tblsp. dry mustard
1 tsp. salt
⅛ tsp. pepper
2 lb. beef round steak, ½" thick
3 tblsp. cooking oil
1 c. thinly sliced pared carrots
½ c. chopped onion
1 (16-oz.) can tomatoes, cut up
1 tblsp. Worcestershire sauce
1 tblsp. brown sugar, packed
¼ c. cold water

Combine flour, mustard, salt and pepper; reserving 2 tblsp.

Pound steak with meat mallet to tenderize. Cut into serving pieces. Coat with remaining flour mixture.

Heat oil in 10" skillet over medium-high heat. Brown steak in hot oil, removing as it browns to 13x9x2" (3-qt.) glass baking dish. Top with carrots and onion. Combine tomatoes, Worcestershire sauce and brown sugar in bowl; pour over meat. Cover with aluminum foil.

Bake in 350° oven 1½ hours, or until meat is tender.

Remove meat from dish; keep warm. Pour vegetable mixture into measuring cup. Add enough water to make 3 c. Pour into 2-qt. saucepan and place over medium heat.

Combine 2 tblsp. reserved flour mixture with ¼ c. cold water in jar. Cover and shake until blended. Stir flour mixture into hot vegetable mixture. Cook, stirring constantly, until mixture boils and thickens. Spoon some gravy over meat. Pass remaining gravy. Makes 6 servings.

Zesty Beef Surprise

2 lb. beef round steak, ¾″ thick
16 saltine crackers, crushed into fine crumbs
⅓ c. flour
½ tsp. garlic salt
½ tsp. onion salt
½ tsp. paprika
1 egg, beaten
1 tblsp. Worcestershire sauce
3 tblsp. cooking oil
1 large onion, sliced
2 (8-oz.) cans tomato sauce
½ c. chili sauce
6 tblsp. brown sugar, packed
¼ c. vinegar
½ tsp. chili powder
½ tsp. dry mustard
1 green pepper, sliced into rings

Cut beef into 8 serving-sized pieces. Combine cracker crumbs, flour, garlic salt, onion salt and paprika in pie plate. Combine egg and Worcestershire sauce in another pie plate. Dip steaks into egg mixture, then into crumb mixture.

Heat oil in 10″ skillet over medium-high heat. Add steaks and brown well on both sides.

Place in 13x9x2″ (3-qt.) glass baking dish. Top with onion. Combine tomato sauce, chili sauce, brown sugar, vinegar, chili powder and mustard in bowl; pour over steaks. Arrange green pepper on top. Cover with aluminum foil.

Bake in 325° oven 2 hours, or until beef is tender. Makes 6 to 8 servings.

3

Texican Chili

6 strips bacon, diced
2 lb. boneless beef round, cut into ½" cubes
2 (15-oz.) cans kidney beans, drained
1 (28-oz.) can tomatoes, cut up
1 (8-oz.) can tomato sauce
1 c. finely chopped onion
½ c. thinly sliced pared carrots
½ c. finely chopped green pepper
½ c. finely chopped celery
2 tblsp. minced fresh parsley
2 cloves garlic, minced
1 bay leaf
2 tblsp. chili powder
1 tsp. salt
½ tsp. ground cumin
⅛ tsp. pepper

Fry bacon in 10" skillet over medium heat 5 minutes, or until browned. Remove bacon with slotted spoon and drain on paper towels.

Brown one half of the beef cubes in pan drippings 5 minutes. Place in 3½-qt. slow cooker. Repeat with remaining beef cubes. Stir bacon and remaining ingredients into slow cooker.

Cover and cook on low setting 10 to 12 hours, or until beef is tender. Makes 6 servings.

Five-Hour Oven Stew

1½ lb. boneless beef round, cut into 1″ cubes
5 medium potatoes, pared and cut into eighths
2 c. cut-up pared carrots, 1″ chunks
1 c. very coarsely chopped onion
1 c. sliced celery, ½″ pieces
2 (14½-oz.) cans stewed tomatoes
2 tblsp. quick-cooking tapioca
1 tblsp. sugar
1½ tsp. salt
⅛ tsp. pepper

Combine all ingredients in large bowl. Mix lightly, but well. Turn into 3-qt. casserole. Cover with lid.

Bake in 275° oven 5 hours, or until meat is tender. Let stand 5 minutes before serving. Makes 6 servings.

Heirloom Beef Stew

2 lb. boneless beef round, cut into 1″ cubes
2 tsp. salt
¼ tsp. pepper
2 tblsp. cooking oil
1 c. chopped onion
½ c. chopped celery
2 c. water
2 beef bouillon cubes
5 medium carrots, pared and cut into 2″ long
   strips (2 c.)
4 c. coarsely chopped cabbage
6 medium potatoes, pared and cut into
   1″ cubes (4 c.)
1 (16-oz.) can tomatoes, cut up
2 tsp. dried marjoram leaves
¼ c. flour
½ c. cold water

Season beef cubes with 1 tsp. of the salt and pepper. Heat oil in 4-qt. Dutch oven over medium-high heat.

Brown beef cubes in hot oil. Add onion and celery; sauté 5 minutes. Add 2 c. water and beef bouillon cubes. Cook until mixture comes to a boil; reduce heat to low. Cover and simmer 45 minutes.

Add carrots, cabbage, potatoes, tomatoes, marjoram and remaining 1 tsp. salt. Simmer, covered, 30 minutes, or until meat and vegetables are tender.

Combine flour and ½ c. cold water in a jar. Cover and shake well to blend. Stir into simmering stew. Cook, stirring constantly, until stew boils and thickens, about 2 minutes. Makes 8 servings.

Pizza Meat Loaf

2 lb. ground lean beef
1 c. soft bread crumbs
1 c. shredded mozzarella cheese (4 oz.)
½ c. finely diced fully cooked ham
2 tblsp. minced fresh parsley
1 small clove garlic, minced
1½ tsp. dried oregano leaves
1 tsp. salt
¼ tsp. pepper
2 eggs, slightly beaten
½ c. tomato juice

Combine all ingredients in large bowl. Mix lightly, but well. Shape mixture into 12" loaf on greased 15½x10½x1" jelly roll pan or shallow roasting pan.

Bake in 350° oven 50 minutes, or until well browned. Let stand 5 minutes before slicing. Makes 6 to 8 servings.

Potato-Frosted Meat Loaf

2 lb. ground beef
2 c. soft bread crumbs
½ c. finely chopped onion
2 tblsp. minced fresh parsley
2 tsp. dried marjoram leaves
2 tsp. salt
¼ tsp. pepper
2 eggs, slightly beaten
1 c. tomato juice
2 lb. all-purpose potatoes, pared and quartered
   (6 medium)
⅓ c. milk
¼ c. butter or regular margarine
1 egg, well beaten
1 c. shredded Cheddar cheese (4 oz.)

Combine ground beef, bread crumbs, onion, parsley, marjoram, salt, pepper, 2 eggs and tomato juice in bowl. Mix lightly, but well. Shape into 9" loaf on greased 15½x10½x1" jelly roll pan or shallow roasting pan.

Bake in 350° oven 50 minutes.

Meanwhile, cook potatoes in 3-qt. saucepan in boiling salted water 25 minutes, or until tender. Drain well.

Heat milk and butter in saucepan over medium heat until butter melts. Mash potatoes with vegetable masher. Add milk-butter mixture, a little at a time, mixing well. Stir in 1 egg. Spread meat loaf with hot potato mixture, then sprinkle with Cheddar cheese.

Place frosted meat loaf under broiler, 9" from source of heat, until cheese melts and surface is lightly browned. Let stand 5 minutes before slicing. Makes 6 to 8 servings.

Tasty Meat Loaf

**2 lb. ground chuck
1 c. coarsely shredded pared carrots
¾ c. quick-cooking oats
½ c. chopped onion
½ c. chopped green pepper
2 tblsp. minced fresh parsley
2 tsp. salt
1 tsp. dried thyme leaves
¼ tsp. pepper
½ c. ketchup
2 tblsp. prepared yellow mustard
2 eggs, slightly beaten
¼ c. milk**

Combine all ingredients in bowl. Mix lightly, but well. Shape mixture into 10″ loaf on 15½x10½x1″ jelly roll pan or shallow roasting pan.

Bake in 350° oven 1 hour 15 minutes, or until well browned. Let stand 10 minutes before slicing. Makes 6 to 8 servings.

Meatball Vegetable Pie

Flaky Pastry (recipe follows)
1 lb. ground beef
¾ c. soft bread crumbs
¼ c. minced onion
2 tblsp. chopped fresh parsley
1 tsp. salt
½ tsp. dried marjoram leaves
1 egg, slightly beaten
2 tblsp. milk
2 tblsp. cooking oil
1 (16-oz.) can stewed tomatoes
1 tblsp. cornstarch
2 beef bouillon cubes
1 c. frozen peas, thawed
1 c. sliced pared carrots, cooked and drained

Prepare Flaky Pastry. Divide dough almost in half. Roll out larger portion of dough on floured surface to ⅛" thickness. Line 10" pie plate with pastry.

Combine next 8 ingredients in bowl. Mix lightly, but well. Shape mixture into 48 meatballs.

Heat oil in 10" skillet over medium heat. Brown meatballs in hot oil. Remove meatballs as they brown and drain on paper towels. Pour off drippings.

Blend together some of tomato liquid with cornstarch in bowl. Add cornstarch mixture, stewed tomatoes and beef bouillon cubes to skillet. Cook, stirring constantly, until mixture boils and thickens. Stir in peas and carrots.

Arrange meatballs in pie shell. Pour vegetable mixture over all. Roll out remaining pastry to ⅛" thickness. Adjust top crust over filling. Seal edges; then flute. Cut vents.

Bake in 400° oven 15 minutes. Reduce heat to 350°; bake 25 minutes more, or until crust is golden brown. Makes 6 servings.

Flaky Pastry: Sift together 2⅔ c. sifted flour and ¾ tsp. salt into bowl. Cut in 1 c. regular margarine until mixture is crumbly, using a pastry blender. Sprinkle with 7 to 8 tblsp. ice water; mix with fork until dough forms.

Beef Skillet Stew

1 lb. ground chuck
½ c. soft bread crumbs
⅓ c. minced onion
2 tblsp. chopped fresh parsley
½ tsp. salt
½ tsp. dried thyme leaves
1 egg, slightly beaten
1 medium onion, sliced
2 (10½-oz.) cans condensed beef broth
3 medium potatoes, pared and cut into
   1″ cubes (1 lb.)
2 c. pared carrot strips, 2″ long
1 (9-oz.) pkg. frozen cut green beans,
   thawed (2 c.)
3 tblsp. cornstarch
¼ c. cold water
1 tsp. browning for gravy

Combine ground chuck, bread crumbs, onion, parsley, salt, thyme and egg in bowl; mix lightly, but well. Shape into 4 (3″) square meat patties.

Cook in 12″ skillet over medium heat 3 minutes. Turn patties; add sliced onion. Cook 3 minutes more. Remove beef patties.

Add enough water to beef broth to make 3 c. Add to onion in skillet with potatoes, carrots and beans. Cover and simmer 8 minutes.

Cut each browned beef patty into 6 cubes. Add to vegetables in skillet. Simmer, covered, 5 minutes more.

Combine cornstarch and ¼ c. cold water in bowl; stir until blended. Stir into hot mixture with browning for gravy. Boil 1 minute, stirring constantly, or until thickened. Makes 4 servings.

Ground Beef-Vegetable Stew

2 lb. ground beef round
½ c. chopped onion
1 clove garlic, minced
1 tblsp. dried parsley flakes
2 tsp. salt
1 tsp. dried basil leaves
½ tsp. pepper
1 (28-oz.) can tomatoes, cut up
6 medium potatoes, pared and cut into
    ¾ " cubes (4 c.)
1 (16-oz.) can pork and beans in tomato sauce
1 (10-oz.) pkg. frozen peas (2 c.)

Brown ground round in 4-qt. Dutch oven over medium-high heat. When meat begins to change color, add onion, garlic, parsley, salt, basil and pepper. Sauté until meat is well browned. Add tomatoes and cook until mixture comes to a boil; reduce heat to low. Cover and simmer 50 minutes, stirring occasionally.

Add potatoes and pork and beans; cook, covered, 20 minutes.

Add peas; cook, covered, 10 minutes more, or until vegetables are tender. Makes 8 servings.

Stuffed Cabbage Bundles

1 c. water
½ c. uncooked regular rice
1 (3-lb.) cabbage
1 lb. ground chuck
1 c. shredded pared carrots
½ c. minced onion
¼ c. minced fresh parsley
1½ tsp. salt
⅛ tsp. pepper
1 egg, slightly beaten
1 c. milk
1 (28-oz.) can tomatoes, cut up
1 (15-oz.) can tomato sauce
1 tsp. dried thyme leaves

Bring 1 c. water to a boil in 2-qt. saucepan over high heat. Add rice. Reduce heat to low; cover and simmer about 15 minutes, or until water is absorbed. Remove from heat; cool completely.

Cut out core of cabbage. Steam cabbage in 1″ boiling water in 4-qt. Dutch oven to soften leaves, about 7 minutes. Remove from water; cool slightly. Pull 16 leaves away gently, one at a time. Drain on paper towels. Trim off thick part of each leaf for easier rolling. If inner leaves need further softening, place cabbage back into boiling water.

Combine cooked rice, ground chuck, carrots, onion, parsley, salt, pepper, egg and milk in bowl. Mix lightly, but well. Place ¼ c. filling on each cabbage leaf; roll up and secure with toothpicks. (Makes 16 bundles.)

Combine tomatoes, tomato sauce and thyme in 4-qt. Dutch oven. Add cabbage bundles and cover. Cook over high heat until mixture comes to a boil; reduce heat to low. Simmer 45 minutes, or until rolls are tender. Makes 8 servings.

Cheese Macaroni Medley

1 c. uncooked elbow macaroni
1 lb. ground beef
½ tsp. salt
¼ tsp. pepper
1 c. chopped onion
1 c. green pepper strips
1 (4-oz.) can sliced mushrooms, drained
2 tblsp. butter or regular margarine
2 tblsp. flour
½ tsp. salt
2 c. milk
3 c. shredded Cheddar cheese (12 oz.)
1 (14½-oz.) can sliced baby tomatoes, drained

Cook elbow macaroni in boiling salted water in 3-qt. saucepan until almost tender, about 12 minutes. Drain well and set aside.

Meanwhile, cook ground beef, ½ tsp. salt and pepper in 12" skillet over medium heat until meat begins to turn color. Add onion, green pepper and mushrooms. Continue to cook until meat is well browned. Drain off excess fat; set aside.

Melt butter in 2-qt. saucepan over medium heat, about 2 minutes. Stir in flour and ½ tsp. salt. Cook 1 minute, stirring constantly. Gradually stir in milk. Cook, stirring constantly, until mixture boils and thickens. Remove from heat.

Add 2½ c. of the Cheddar cheese and stir until cheese is melted. Combine cheese sauce with meat mixture in skillet. Add macaroni; mix gently. Turn into 12x8x2" (2-qt.) glass baking dish. Top with sliced baby tomatoes and remaining ½ c. Cheddar cheese.

Bake in 350° oven 30 minutes, or until hot and bubbly. Makes 8 servings.

Beef 'n' Stuffing Squares

¼ c. butter or regular margarine
2 c. chopped celery and leaves
1 c. chopped onion
8 c. cubed fresh bread, ¼"
1 lb. ground beef
¼ c. chopped fresh parsley
2 tsp. rubbed sage
¼ tsp. pepper
2 eggs, slightly beaten
1 (10½-oz.) can condensed beef broth
½ c. milk
Easy Mushroom Gravy (recipe follows)

Melt butter in 10" skillet over medium heat, about 2 minutes. Add celery and onion and sauté until tender. Combine sautéed vegetables, bread cubes, ground beef, parsley, sage, pepper, eggs, beef broth and milk in bowl. Mix lightly, but well. Press ground beef mixture into greased 12x8x2" (2-qt.) glass baking dish.

Bake in 350° oven 40 minutes, or until top is golden brown. Cut into 8 squares. Prepare Easy Mushroom Gravy and serve over squares. Makes 8 servings.

Easy Mushroom Gravy: Combine 1½ c. beef broth, 1 (4-oz.) can sliced mushrooms (drained), 2 tsp. Worcestershire sauce and ¼ tsp. browning for gravy in 2-qt. saucepan. Cook over medium heat until mixture comes to a boil. Combine 3 tblsp. cornstarch and 3 tblsp. cold water in bowl; stir to blend. Gradually stir cornstarch mixture into boiling liquid. Boil 1 minute, stirring constantly. Makes about 2 cups.

15

Two Bean-Beef Bake

1 (10-oz.) pkg. frozen lima beans
1 lb. ground beef
½ c. chopped celery
½ c. chopped green pepper
½ c. chopped onion
2 (16-oz.) cans pork and beans in tomato sauce
1 (6-oz.) can tomato paste
1 c. water
1 tblsp. chili powder
½ tsp. salt
Tortilla chips

Cook lima beans in boiling salted water in 2-qt. saucepan until almost tender. Drain well and set aside.

Meanwhile, cook ground beef in 12" skillet over medium heat until meat begins to turn color. Add celery, green pepper and onion. Cook until meat is well browned.

Stir in cooked lima beans, pork and beans, tomato paste, water, chili powder and salt. Turn mixture into 2-qt. casserole.

Bake in 350° oven 30 minutes, or until hot and bubbly. Before serving, garnish with a border of tortilla chips. Makes 8 servings.

Dinner in a Dish

3 c. stiff, hot mashed potatoes*
1 egg, beaten
1 lb. ground beef
½ c. chopped onion
2 tblsp. chopped fresh parsley
1 tsp. dried marjoram leaves
½ tsp. salt
¼ tsp. pepper
2 tblsp. flour
1 (16-oz.) can tomatoes, cut up
1½ c. frozen peas, thawed
½ c. ketchup
2 beef bouillon cubes

Combine mashed potatoes with egg in bowl. Mix well; set aside.

Cook ground beef, onion, parsley, marjoram, salt and pepper in 10″ skillet over medium heat until well browned.

Drain off excess fat. Stir in flour. Add tomatoes, peas, ketchup and beef bouillon cubes. Cook until mixture comes to a boil, stirring constantly. Pour into 2-qt. casserole. Top with potato mixture, making 8 mounds.

Bake in 350° oven 35 minutes, or until potatoes are golden brown. Makes 8 servings.

*Note: Fresh or instant mashed potatoes can be used. If instant are used, prepare according to package directions for 6 servings, adding additional dry flakes to make stiff mashed potatoes.

Beef-Carrot Casserole

1 tblsp. butter or regular margarine
1 lb. ground beef
¼ c. minced onion
1 clove garlic, minced
2 (8-oz.) cans tomato sauce
1 tsp. salt
¼ tsp. pepper
1 c. dairy sour cream
1 c. creamed small curd cottage cheese
1 c. sliced pared carrots, cooked and drained
¼ c. chopped fresh parsley
8 oz. medium noodles, cooked and drained
1 c. shredded Cheddar cheese (4 oz.)

Melt butter in 10″ skillet over medium heat. Add ground beef and cook until meat begins to turn color. Add onion and garlic. Sauté until meat is well browned. Stir in tomato sauce, salt and pepper. Reduce heat to low and simmer 5 minutes.

Combine sour cream, cottage cheese, carrots and parsley in bowl. Add cooked noodles; mix well.

Alternate layers of the meat mixture and noodle mixture in greased 3-qt. casserole, beginning and ending with noodle mixture. Top with Cheddar cheese.

Bake in 350° oven 30 minutes, or until hot and bubbly. Makes 6 to 8 servings.

Barbecued Beef Patties

1 lb. ground beef
1 c. soft bread crumbs
1 tblsp. chopped onion
1 tsp. salt
½ tsp. dried marjoram leaves
⅛ tsp. pepper
½ c. milk
½ c. ketchup
½ c. water
½ c. chopped green pepper
½ c. chopped onion
3 tblsp. vinegar
1½ tblsp. Worcestershire sauce
1 tblsp. sugar

Combine ground beef, bread crumbs, 1 tblsp. onion, salt, marjoram, pepper and milk in bowl. Mix lightly, but well. Shape mixture into four patties. Place in greased 9″ square baking pan.

Combine ketchup, water, green pepper, ½ c. onion, vinegar, Worcestershire sauce and sugar in bowl; mix well. Pour over beef patties.

Bake in 375° oven 1 hour, or until hot and bubbly. Makes 4 servings.

19

Rosemary Lamb Stew

2 lb. boneless lamb shoulder
2 tsp. salt
2 tblsp. cooking oil
½ c. water
3 medium potatoes, pared and cut into
   1″ cubes
2 c. thinly sliced pared carrots
1 c. finely chopped onion
¼ c. chopped fresh parsley
1 clove garlic, minced
1 tsp. dried rosemary leaves
¼ tsp. pepper
2 tblsp. cornstarch
½ c. cold water

Trim excess fat from lamb and cut into 1″ cubes. Season lamb with 1 tsp. of the salt.

Heat oil in 12″ skillet over medium-high heat. Brown lamb cubes in hot oil 10 minutes. Stir in ½ c. water. Cook until mixture comes to a boil, stirring to loosen browned particles in bottom of skillet. Pour hot lamb mixture into 3½-qt. slow cooker.

Stir in remaining 1 tsp. salt, potatoes, carrots, onion, parsley, garlic, rosemary and pepper. Cover and cook on low setting 9 to 10 hours, or until lamb and potatoes are tender.

Combine cornstarch and ½ c. cold water in bowl; stir to blend. Stir into stew. Turn heat to high setting. Cover and cook until mixture thickens, about 15 minutes. Makes 4 to 6 servings.

Deep-Dish Pork Pie

Pastry for 1-crust (9") pie
$1/_{16}$ tsp. dried thyme leaves
3 tblsp. butter or regular margarine
1 c. chopped green pepper
¼ c. chopped onion
3 tblsp. flour
1 tsp. salt
¼ tsp. ground ginger
$1/_8$ tsp. dry mustard
1½ c. chicken broth
½ tsp. browning for gravy
3 c. cubed cooked pork, ¾"
3 c. sliced pared carrots, cooked and drained

Prepare pastry, adding thyme to flour mixture. Set aside.

Melt butter in 10" skillet over medium heat, about 2 minutes. Add green pepper and onion; sauté until tender. Add flour, salt, ginger and mustard. Cook 1 minute, stirring constantly. Gradually stir in chicken broth. Cook, stirring constantly, until mixture boils and thickens.

Add browning for gravy to skillet; stir well. Stir in pork and carrots. Turn mixture into 2-qt. casserole.

Roll out pastry on floured surface to fit top of casserole. Adjust pastry over filling. Seal edges; then flute. Cut vents.

Bake in 400° oven 35 minutes, or until crust is golden brown. Makes 6 servings.

Two-Step Bean Cassoulet

1 lb. dried navy beans
6 c. water
12 strips bacon, diced
1 lb. boneless pork, cut into ½" cubes
1 c. finely chopped onion
2 cloves garlic, minced
1 bay leaf
¾ tsp. dried thyme leaves
½ tsp. salt
⅛ tsp. pepper

Wash navy beans thoroughly. Soak navy beans overnight in 6 c. water in 3½-qt. slow cooker.

The next day, cover and cook on high setting 3 hours, or until beans are tender. Drain beans in colander, reserving 2 c. cooking liquid.

Fry bacon in 10" skillet over medium heat 5 minutes, or until browned. Remove bacon with slotted spoon and drain on paper towels.

Brown pork cubes in pan drippings 5 minutes. Combine beans, bacon, pork, 2 c. reserved cooking liquid and remaining ingredients in slow cooker.

Cover and cook on low setting 5 hours, or until pork is tender. Makes 6 to 8 servings.

Wisconsin Lumberjack Stew

2 lb. boneless pork, cut into 1" cubes
1 tsp. salt
1 tsp. sugar
½ tsp. paprika
½ tsp. pepper
2 tblsp. cooking oil
1 c. sliced onion
1 clove garlic, minced
3 c. water
1 tblsp. lemon juice
1 tsp. Worcestershire sauce
2 bay leaves
2 chicken bouillon cubes
6 medium carrots, pared and cut into
    1" chunks (2 c.)
1 lb. small white onions, peeled
2 (9-oz.) pkg. frozen cut green beans
3 tblsp. cornstarch
½ c. cold water

Season pork with salt, sugar, paprika and pepper. Heat oil in 4-qt. Dutch oven over medium-high heat. Brown pork in hot oil.

Add sliced onion and garlic; sauté 5 minutes. Add water, lemon juice, Worcestershire sauce, bay leaves and chicken bouillon cubes. Cook until mixture comes to a boil; reduce heat to low. Cover and simmer 1 hour.

Add carrots and whole onions; simmer, covered, 40 minutes.

Add green beans; simmer, covered, 10 minutes, or until meat and vegetables are tender.

Combine cornstarch and ½ c. cold water in bowl; stir to blend. Stir into simmering stew. Cook, stirring constantly, until stew boils and thickens, about 2 minutes. Makes 8 servings.

Ham and Pork Loaf

1 lb. ground fully cooked ham
1 lb. ground pork
2 c. cooked regular rice
½ c. finely chopped onion
1 tblsp. minced fresh parsley
1 tsp. salt
¼ tsp. pepper
¼ tsp. ground cloves
2 eggs, slightly beaten
½ c. milk
Mustard-Egg Sauce (recipe follows)

Combine ham, pork, rice, onion, parsley, salt, pepper, cloves, eggs and milk in large bowl. Mix lightly, but well. Shape mixture into a 10″ loaf on a greased 15½x10½x1″ jelly roll pan or shallow roasting pan.

Bake in 350° oven 1 hour 15 minutes, or until golden brown. Let stand 5 minutes before slicing. Prepare Mustard-Egg Sauce. Pass Mustard-Egg Sauce with meat loaf. Makes 6 to 8 servings.

Mustard-Egg Sauce: Melt ¼ c. butter or regular margarine in 2-qt. saucepan over medium heat. Stir in ¼ c. flour, 1 tsp. dry mustard, ½ tsp. salt and ⅛ tsp. pepper. Cook 1 minute, stirring constantly. Gradually stir in 2 c. milk. Cook, stirring constantly, until mixture boils and thickens. Add 2 chopped hard-cooked eggs. Heat well.

Freeze-Ahead Ham Loaves

6 c. ground fully cooked ham
1 c. soft bread crumbs
2 eggs, slightly beaten
¼ c. finely chopped celery
¼ c. finely chopped onion
¼ tsp. dry mustard
⅛ tsp. pepper
1 c. apple juice
½ c. milk
Pineapple Glaze (recipe follows)

Combine ground ham, bread crumbs, eggs, celery, onion, dry mustard, pepper, apple juice and milk in bowl. Mix lightly, but well. Shape into 8 small loaves. Place on waxed paper-lined baking sheet. Freeze 2 hours, or until firm. Wrap loaves in aluminum foil. Freeze up to 4 weeks.

To bake, arrange frozen ham loaves on 15½x10½x1″ jelly roll pan or shallow roasting pan.

Bake in 350° oven 30 minutes.

While loaves are baking, prepare Pineapple Glaze.

Remove ham loaves from oven; pour off pan drippings. Arrange 3 pineapple pieces on top of each loaf. Brush Pineapple Glaze over loaves, using one half of glaze.

Bake 15 minutes more. Brush with remaining Pineapple Glaze. Bake 15 minutes more, or until golden brown. Makes 8 servings.

Pineapple Glaze: Drain 1 (8¼-oz.) can sliced pineapple in juice, reserving juice. Cut each pineapple slice into 6 pieces; set aside. Combine 1 tblsp. brown sugar (packed), 1 tblsp. cornstarch and dash of ground cloves in saucepan. Stir in reserved pineapple juice, 1 tblsp. lemon juice and ½ c. water. Cook over medium heat, stirring constantly, until it boils and thickens. Keep warm.

Ham Casserole au Gratin

1 c. uncooked elbow macaroni
½ c. butter or regular margarine
¾ c. chopped celery
½ c. chopped onion
1 (10¾-oz.) can condensed cream of chicken
  soup
1½ c. milk
1½ c. shredded Cheddar cheese (6 oz.)
1 c. cubed fully cooked ham, ½″
4 hard-cooked eggs, chopped
½ c. soft bread crumbs
¼ c. chopped pimientos
½ c. saltine cracker crumbs
1 tblsp. butter or regular margarine, melted

Cook macaroni in boiling salted water in 4-qt. Dutch oven until almost tender. Drain. Rinse with cold water. Drain well; set aside.

Melt ½ c. butter in 3-qt. saucepan over medium heat. Add celery and onion and sauté until tender. Add cream of chicken soup. Gradually stir in milk. Slowly add Cheddar cheese, stirring constantly, until melted. Remove from heat.

Add ham, eggs, bread crumbs and pimientos to sauce; mix well. Turn into greased 12x8x2″ (2-qt.) glass baking dish. Combine cracker crumbs and 1 tblsp. melted butter in bowl. Sprinkle on top.

Bake in 350° oven 30 minutes, or until hot and bubbly. Makes 6 servings.

Lasagne Spinach Roll-Ups

1 (28-oz.) can Italian tomatoes
1 lb. bulk pork sausage
1 c. chopped onion
2 cloves garlic, minced
2 (6-oz.) cans tomato paste
1½ c. water
2 (4-oz.) cans mushroom stems and pieces, drained
¼ c. chopped fresh parsley
1 tsp. dried oregano leaves
1 tsp. dried basil leaves
¼ tsp. pepper
2 dashes Tabasco sauce
1 bay leaf
2 (10-oz.) pkg. frozen chopped spinach, thawed
1 (15-oz.) carton ricotta cheese
2 c. shredded mozzarella cheese (8 oz.)
2 eggs, slightly beaten
6 tblsp. grated Romano cheese
½ tsp. salt
⅛ tsp. ground nutmeg
12 lasagne noodles, cooked and drained

Purée Italian tomatoes in blender until smooth; set aside.

Cook sausage, onion and garlic in 4-qt. Dutch oven over medium heat until meat is browned. Stir in puréed tomatoes, tomato paste, water, mushrooms, 2 tblsp. of the parsley, oregano, basil, pepper, Tabasco sauce and bay leaf. Cook until mixture comes to a boil; reduce heat to low. Simmer, partially covered, 45 minutes. Remove bay leaf.

Drain and press liquid from thawed spinach in sieve. Combine spinach, remaining 2 tblsp. parsley, ricotta cheese, mozzarella cheese, eggs, 4 tblsp. of the Romano cheese, salt and nutmeg in bowl; mix well. Spread ⅓ c. filling on each noodle; roll up.

Place 1½ c. sauce in 13x9x2" (3-qt.) glass baking dish. Arrange stuffed noodles in dish, seam side down. Top with remaining sauce and remaining 2 tblsp. Romano cheese.

Bake in 350° oven 30 minutes, or until hot and bubbly. Let stand 10 minutes before serving. Makes 6 servings.

Chili-Bologna Bake

4 strips bacon, diced
1 c. chopped onion
1 c. chopped green pepper
1 clove garlic, minced
2 (16-oz.) cans red kidney beans, drained
2 (15-oz.) cans chili with beans
1½ lb. unsliced regular bologna, cut into
   1″ cubes
1 c. sliced ripe olives
1 (4-oz.) jar pimientos, chopped and drained
1 c. shredded Cheddar cheese (4 oz.)

Fry bacon in 10″ skillet over medium heat until partially cooked. Add onion, green pepper and garlic; sauté until tender.

Combine kidney beans, chili with beans, bologna, olives, pimientos and sautéed mixture in bowl; mix well. Turn into 3-qt. casserole. Cover with aluminum foil.

Bake in 350° oven 45 minutes.

Remove foil. Sprinkle with Cheddar cheese. Bake 10 minutes more, or until cheese is melted. Makes 6 to 8 servings.

Super Chicken Casserole

1 (3-lb.) broiler-fryer, cut up
4 c. water
1 c. chopped onion
1 tsp. salt
¼ tsp. pepper
1 tsp. salt
2 c. uncooked medium noodles
1 (8-oz.) can sliced mushrooms
3 hard-cooked eggs, chopped
1¼ c. milk
1 (10¾-oz.) can condensed cream of mushroom
   soup
¾ c. soft bread crumbs
2 tblsp. butter or regular margarine, melted

Place broiler-fryer, water, onion, 1 tsp. salt and pepper in 4-qt. Dutch oven. Cook over high heat until mixture comes to a boil; reduce heat to low. Cover and simmer 1 hour, or until chicken is tender. Remove chicken from broth. Reserve 2 c. of chicken broth. Cool chicken until it can be handled.

Remove meat from bones and cut into chunks. Discard skin and bones. Set chicken aside.

Place reserved 2 c. chicken broth and 1 tsp. salt in 2-qt. saucepan. Cook over high heat until it comes to a boil. Add noodles and cook 4 minutes, or until almost tender. (All the chicken broth will be absorbed.)

Drain mushrooms, reserving liquid. Place one half of noodles in greased 13x9x2″ (3-qt.) glass baking dish. Top with one half of eggs, then one half of mushrooms and one half of chicken. Repeat layers.

Gradually stir milk into cream of mushroom soup in bowl; blend well. Stir in reserved mushroom liquid. Pour soup mixture over casserole mixture. Toss bread crumbs with melted butter in bowl. Sprinkle over top.

Bake in 350° oven 25 minutes, or until hot and bubbly. Makes 6 servings.

Chicken Lima Bean Stew

1 (3-lb.) broiler-fryer, cut up
4 c. water
2 tblsp. minced fresh parsley
¾ tsp. poultry seasoning
¼ tsp. pepper
4 chicken bouillon cubes
Dumplings (recipe follows)
¼ c. cornstarch
½ c. cold water
1 (17-oz.) can whole-kernel corn
2 c. thinly sliced onion
1½ c. thinly sliced pared carrots
1 (10-oz.) pkg. frozen lima beans

Place chicken, 4 c. water, parsley, poultry seasoning, pepper and chicken bouillon cubes in 4-qt. Dutch oven. Cook over high heat until mixture comes to a boil; reduce heat to low. Cover and simmer 1 hour, or until chicken is tender.

Remove chicken from broth. Cool chicken until it can be handled. Remove meat from bones. Cut chicken into large pieces. Discard skin and bones.

Prepare Dumplings; set aside.

Blend together cornstarch and ½ c. cold water in bowl; stir to blend. Cook broth over high heat until mixture comes to a boil.

Stir cornstarch mixture into simmering broth; cook 1 minute, stirring constantly, until thickened. Add undrained corn, onion, carrots, lima beans and chicken. Drop Dumplings in 12 spoonfuls on top of simmering stew. Cook, uncovered, 10 minutes.

Cover and cook 10 minutes more, or until dumplings are light and fluffy. Makes 8 servings.

Dumplings: Combine 2 c. buttermilk baking mix, 2 tblsp. chopped fresh parsley and ⅔ c. milk in bowl. Stir just until moistened.

Oven-Barbecued Chicken

2 tblsp. cooking oil
½ c. chopped onion
½ c. chopped celery
1 (10½-oz.) can condensed tomato soup
1 c. ketchup
½ c. water
¼ c. lemon juice
3 tblsp. Worcestershire sauce
3 tblsp. brown sugar, packed
2 tblsp. vinegar
2 tblsp. prepared yellow mustard
1½ tsp. salt
¼ tsp. pepper
2 drops Tabasco sauce
2 (2½-lb.) broiler-fryers, quartered

Heat oil in 3-qt. saucepan over medium heat, about 2 minutes. Add onion and celery and sauté until tender. Add tomato soup, ketchup, water, lemon juice, Worcestershire sauce, brown sugar, vinegar, mustard, salt, pepper and Tabasco sauce. Cook until mixture comes to a boil; reduce heat to low. Simmer, uncovered, 30 minutes.

Place chicken in shallow roasting pan. Bake in 400° oven 40 minutes. Baste with barbecue sauce. Continue baking and basting with sauce 20 minutes more, or until chicken is crisp and tender. Makes 8 servings.

Sunday Special Chicken

3 whole chicken breasts, split (about
   12 oz. each)
1/3 c. flour
1/2 tsp. salt
1/2 c. cooking oil
1/2 c. dairy sour cream
3/4 c. bacon-flavored bits
2/3 c. orange marmalade
1/3 c. maple syrup

Coat chicken breasts with a mixture of flour and salt. Heat oil in 12" skillet over medium heat. Brown chicken on all sides in hot oil. As chicken browns, remove and place in 13x9x2" baking pan. Combine sour cream, bacon-flavored bits, marmalade and maple syrup in bowl; mix well. Brush mixture over chicken.

Bake in 350° oven 45 minutes, or until chicken is tender. Makes 6 servings.

Chicken Supreme

1 c. soft bread crumbs
½ c. grated Parmesan cheese
4 whole chicken breasts, split (about
    12 oz. each)
1 c. butter or regular margarine, melted

Combine bread crumbs and Parmesan cheese in bowl. Dip chicken breasts in melted butter, then roll in bread crumb mixture. Arrange chicken breasts in 15½x10½x1" jelly roll pan or shallow roasting pan. Pour remaining butter over chicken and sprinkle with any remaining bread crumb mixture.

Bake in 350° oven 30 minutes. Baste with drippings. Bake 30 minutes more, or until chicken is tender. Makes 8 servings.

Herbed Chicken Cacciatore

> 4 tblsp. cooking oil
> 1 c. finely chopped onion
> ½ c. finely chopped green pepper
> 1 clove garlic, minced
> 1 (8-oz.) can tomato sauce
> 1 (6-oz.) can tomato paste
> 1 bay leaf
> ½ tsp. dried thyme leaves
> ½ tsp. dried oregano leaves
> 8 chicken thighs (about 2 lb.)
> 1 tsp. salt
> 1 (4-oz.) can sliced mushrooms, drained
> Hot cooked spaghetti

Heat 2 tblsp. of the oil in 12″ skillet over medium heat. Add onion, green pepper and garlic; sauté 5 minutes, or until tender. Combine sautéed vegetables, tomato sauce, tomato paste, bay leaf, thyme and oregano in 3½-qt. slow cooker.

Season chicken thighs with salt. Heat remaining oil in same skillet over medium heat. Add chicken thighs and cook until browned, about 10 minutes. Place in slow cooker.

Cover and cook on low setting 6 hours, or until chicken is tender. Stir in mushrooms. Cover and cook on high setting 15 minutes more. Serve over spaghetti. Makes 4 servings.

Chicken-Ham Casserole

6 tblsp. butter or regular margarine
5 tblsp. flour
$\frac{1}{2}$ tsp. salt
$\frac{1}{4}$ tsp. pepper
2 c. light cream
1 c. chicken broth
1 c. grated Parmesan cheese
8 oz. spaghetti, cooked and drained
2 c. cubed cooked chicken, 1″
2 c. cubed fully cooked ham, 1″
2 (4-oz.) cans sliced mushrooms
1 (10-oz.) pkg. frozen peas, thawed (2 c.)

Melt butter in 3-qt. saucepan over medium heat. Blend in flour, salt and pepper; cook, stirring constantly, 1 minute. Stir in light cream and chicken broth. Cook over medium heat, stirring constantly, until mixture boils and thickens. Stir in $\frac{1}{2}$ c. of the Parmesan cheese.

Combine spaghetti, chicken, ham, undrained mushrooms, peas and cheese sauce in bowl; toss gently to mix. Turn into 3-qt. casserole. Sprinkle with remaining $\frac{1}{2}$ c. Parmesan cheese.

Bake in 350° oven 30 minutes, or until hot and bubbly. Makes 8 servings.

Mexican Enchiladas

2 tblsp. butter or regular margarine
½ c. chopped onion
1 (4-oz.) can sliced mushrooms, drained
1 clove garlic, minced
1½ c. finely chopped cooked chicken
1 (4-oz.) can green chilies, drained and chopped
3 c. dairy sour cream
1½ tsp. chili powder
1 tsp. ground cumin
½ tsp. salt
¼ tsp. pepper
Cooking oil
18 tortillas, canned or frozen and thawed
4 c. shredded Cheddar cheese (1 lb.)

Melt butter in 10" skillet over medium heat, about 2 minutes. Add onion, mushrooms and garlic and sauté until tender. Add chicken, chilies, 1 c. of the sour cream, chili powder, cumin, salt and pepper. Heat over low heat, stirring frequently, until hot. (Do not boil.) Remove from heat.

Meanwhile, pour oil into 8" skillet, filling about ½" deep. Heat oil over medium heat until hot. Fry tortillas, one at a time, in hot oil until soft (about 3 seconds each). Drain on paper towels.

Spread a heaping tablespoon of filling in center of each tortilla. Sprinkle each with Cheddar cheese using 2 c. of the cheese. Fold sides over filling. Place seam side down in 13x9x2" (3-qt.) glass baking dish.

Bake in 350° oven 15 minutes. Spread with remaining 2 c. sour cream and sprinkle with remaining 2 c. Cheddar cheese. Bake 8 minutes more, or just until cheese is melted. Makes 6 servings.

Tuna-Cheese Casserole

1 (8-oz.) pkg. shell macaroni
1 (8-oz.) pkg. cream cheese, softened
½ c. dairy sour cream
½ c. creamed small curd cottage cheese
¼ c. sliced green onions and tops
¼ tsp. garlic salt
1 (7-oz.) can tuna, drained and broken into
chunks
2 medium tomatoes, peeled and sliced
¼ tsp. salt
1½ c. shredded sharp process American
cheese (6 oz.)

Cook shell macaroni in boiling salted water in 4-qt. Dutch oven until tender. Drain well.

Meanwhile, stir together cream cheese, sour cream, cottage cheese, green onions and garlic salt in bowl.

Place one half of hot macaroni in bottom of greased 2-qt. casserole. Top with one half of the cream cheese mixture, all of the tuna, remaining macaroni, then remaining cream cheese mixture. Arrange sliced tomatoes on top; sprinkle with salt.

Bake in 350° oven 30 minutes.

Sprinkle American cheese over tomatoes. Continue baking 3 to 5 minutes, or until cheese is melted. Makes 6 to 8 servings.

Pastry-Topped Tuna Pie

Pastry for 1-crust (9″) pie
1 c. pared carrot strips, 2x¼″ long
2 medium onions, quartered
¼ tsp. salt
1 c. frozen peas
¼ c. butter or regular margarine
¼ c. flour
½ tsp. salt
$^1/_{16}$ tsp. pepper
2 c. milk
1 tsp. Worcestershire sauce
2 (7-oz.) cans solid pack tuna, drained and
   broken into chunks
1 (8-oz.) can whole-kernel corn, drained
1 egg yolk, slightly beaten
1 tblsp. water

Prepare pastry; set aside.

Cook carrot strips and onions with ¼ tsp. salt in 1″ boiling water in 3-qt. covered saucepan 8 minutes. Add peas; cover and cook 5 minutes more. Rinse with cold water; drain well.

Melt butter in 3-qt. saucepan over medium heat. Stir in flour, ½ tsp. salt and pepper; cook 1 minute, stirring constantly. Gradually stir in milk and Worcestershire sauce. Cook, stirring constantly, until mixture boils and thickens. Add tuna, corn and cooked vegetables; mix well. Turn into 1½-qt. casserole.

Roll out pastry on floured surface to fit top of casserole. Adjust pastry over filling. Seal edges; then flute. Cut vents. Brush pastry with combined egg yolk and water.

Bake in 400° oven 35 minutes, or until crust is golden brown. Makes 6 servings.

Chapter Two

Tasty Luncheon Specials

You'll find lunch couldn't be easier than when planned around the popular American soup-and-sandwich combination. Lots of farm women tell us that they turn to homemade soup often, no matter what the season, because soup satisfies hearty appetites and stretches the food dollar.

Whether you're looking for a soup or chowder that simmers for hours or is assembled in minutes, we give you 13 deliciously different recipes to choose from. If your family likes a good basic soup, try Chicken-Vegetable Soup made with a whole chicken simmered gently with carrots, parsley, onion and celery. It's seasoned with saffron and lemon juice and enriched with eggs. However, if you need a meal in minutes, make Turkey Corn Chowder featuring potatoes, onion, corn, light cream and leftover turkey. For a change, substitute tuna or chicken for the turkey.

We've got hot sandwich favorites like Barbecued Beef Buns or Pizza Burgers. For Beef Stroganoff Sandwiches, a French loaf is filled with a ground beef mixture laced with sour cream, onion and parsley and topped with melted American cheese. Sandwich traditionalists will like our Grilled Reuben made with layer upon layer of chicken or turkey, boiled ham, Swiss cheese and sauerkraut with Russian dressing between pumpernickel bread slices.

If you like club sandwiches for summertime, serve our Tuna Club—three slices of toast filled with cucumbers, hard-cooked egg and tuna salad. Light, but satisfying.

If your family prefers a hot dish for lunch, serve rich and creamy Macaroni-Cheese Bake. Or how about a Crustless Bacon Quiche that is quickly mixed in a blender and baked in a pie plate?

No matter which recipe you use, you can turn an everyday lunch into something special.

Hearty Tomato-Beef Soup

1 tblsp. butter or regular margarine
1 lb. ground beef
1 c. chopped onion
½ c. chopped celery
1 (28-oz.) can tomatoes, cut up
2 beef bouillon cubes
⅓ c. uncooked regular rice
1 tsp. salt
½ tsp. chili powder
1 bay leaf
2½ c. water

Melt butter in 4-qt. Dutch oven over medium heat, about 2 minutes. Add ground beef, onion and celery and cook until meat is well browned.

Stir in tomatoes, beef bouillon cubes, rice, salt, chili powder, bay leaf and water. Cook over high heat until it comes to a boil; reduce heat to low. Cover and simmer 20 minutes.

Remove bay leaf before serving. Makes 2 quarts.

Chicken-Vegetable Soup

1 (3-lb.) broiler-fryer, quartered
2 qt. water
4 medium onions, quartered
4 stalks celery, cut into 3" chunks
3 medium pared carrots, cut into 3" chunks
10 sprigs fresh parsley
1 tblsp. salt
1 clove garlic
1 bay leaf
½ tsp. dried thyme leaves
2 whole cloves
¼ tsp. pepper
$\frac{1}{16}$ tsp. powdered saffron
1 c. sliced pared carrot
1 c. sliced celery
2 eggs, well beaten
1 tblsp. lemon juice
Sliced green onions and tops
Dairy sour cream

Place chicken, water, onions, celery chunks, carrot chunks, parsley, salt, garlic, bay leaf, thyme, cloves, pepper and saffron in 6-qt. Dutch oven. Cook over high heat until it comes to a boil; reduce heat to low. Cover and simmer 1 hour 15 minutes.

Remove from heat. Strain broth. Pour broth back into Dutch oven. Boil over high heat 15 minutes. Add 1 c. carrot and 1 c. celery. Cover; simmer 10 minutes, or until vegetables are tender. Meanwhile, remove chicken from bones. Cut chicken into chunks and add to broth.

Remove from heat. Let stand 10 minutes. Gradually add 2 c. hot broth to eggs in bowl, stirring vigorously. Slowly stir egg mixture into soup. Add lemon juice. Serve in bowls topped with green onions and sour cream. Makes 2 quarts.

Turkey Corn Chowder

8 strips bacon
2 c. chopped onion
4 c. sliced pared potatoes (¼″ thick)
1 (10¾-oz.) can condensed chicken broth
½ tsp. salt
4 c. cubed cooked turkey
1 (17-oz.) can whole-kernel corn
1 (17-oz.) can cream-style corn
2 c. light cream
¼ tsp. pepper
Chopped fresh parsley

Fry bacon in 4-qt. Dutch oven or saucepan over medium heat until browned. Remove and drain on paper towels. Crumble bacon; set aside.

Pour off all but ¼ c. drippings; sauté onion in ¼ c. drippings over medium heat until tender.

Add potatoes, chicken broth and salt. Cook over high heat until it comes to a boil; reduce heat to low. Cover and simmer 10 minutes, or until potatoes are tender.

Add turkey, undrained corn, cream-style corn, light cream and pepper. Heat thoroughly. Garnish each bowl of soup with bacon bits and parsley. Makes about 3 quarts.

Lamb Noodle Soup

**2½ lb. lamb shoulder, cut in 1½" thick slices
2 tblsp. cooking oil
2 c. chopped celery
1 c. chopped onion
1 clove garlic, minced
7 c. water
1 tblsp. salt
½ tsp. dried thyme leaves
¼ tsp. dried rosemary leaves
¼ tsp. pepper
1 bay leaf
6 oz. uncooked wide noodles (4 c.)
⅓ c. chopped fresh parsley
Sliced green onions and tops**

Remove most of fat from lamb. Heat oil in 4-qt. Dutch oven over medium heat 2 minutes, or until hot.

Add lamb and brown on both sides. Remove and set aside. Add celery, onion and garlic to drippings in Dutch oven; sauté until lightly browned. Add lamb, water, salt, thyme, rosemary, pepper and bay leaf. Cook over high heat until mixture comes to a boil; reduce heat to low. Skim off foam. Cover and simmer 2 hours, or until meat is tender.

Remove lamb from broth. Return broth to a boil over high heat. Add noodles; cover and cook over low heat 15 minutes, or until noodles are tender.

Meanwhile, remove meat from bones and cut into chunks. Add meat and parsley to broth. Serve in bowls topped with green onions. Makes 2 quarts.

Southwestern Chowder

2 strips bacon, diced
1 c. chopped onion
½ lb. ground beef
1 (28-oz.) can tomatoes, cut up
2½ c. water
1 (15-oz.) can kidney beans
3 beef bouillon cubes
1 tsp. chili powder
½ tsp. salt
⅛ tsp. pepper
3 c. hot cooked rice

Partially cook bacon in 4-qt. Dutch oven over medium heat. Add onion and ground beef; cook until onion is tender and meat is browned.

Add tomatoes, water, kidney beans, beef bouillon cubes, chili powder, salt and pepper. Cook over high heat until mixture comes to a boil; reduce heat to low. Cover and simmer 15 minutes.

To serve chowder, place ½ c. rice in each of 6 soup bowls. Ladle in chowder. Makes 6 servings.

Maine Corn Chowder

5 strips bacon, diced
2 medium onions, sliced
3 c. diced pared potatoes
2 c. water
1 tsp. salt
$1/8$ tsp. pepper
1 (17-oz.) can cream-style corn
2 c. milk

Fry bacon in 4-qt. Dutch oven or saucepan over medium heat until browned. Remove with slotted spoon and drain on paper towels. Set aside.

Sauté onion in bacon drippings until tender. Add potatoes, water, salt and pepper. Cook over high heat until mixture comes to a boil; reduce heat to low. Cover and simmer 12 to 15 minutes, or until potatoes are tender.

Add corn and milk; heat thoroughly. Garnish with bacon. Makes about 9 cups.

Green Bean Soup

1 meaty ham bone, about 2 lb.
2 qt. water
4 c. cut-up green beans (1″ pieces)
3 c. cubed pared potatoes
2 medium onions, sliced
¼ c. chopped fresh parsley
1 tsp. dried savory leaves
1 tsp. salt
¼ tsp. pepper
1 c. light cream

Place ham bone and water in 6-qt. Dutch oven. Cook over high heat until it comes to a boil. Reduce heat to low; cover and simmer 1½ hours, or until meat is tender.

Remove bone from liquid. Remove meat from bone and cut into chunks. Return meat to cooking liquid.

Add green beans, potatoes, onions, parsley, savory, salt and pepper. Cook over high heat until mixture comes to a boil; reduce heat to low. Cover and simmer 20 minutes, or until vegetables are tender. Skim off excess fat.

Just before serving, stir in light cream. Makes about 3½ quarts.

Espanola Valley Soup

3 lb. fresh pork hocks
3 qt. water
1 (16-oz.) can tomatoes, cut up
2 c. chopped onion
1 clove garlic, minced
5 tsp. salt
1 tblsp. chili powder
2 (16-oz.) cans whole-kernel corn or hominy
1 (10-oz.) pkg. frozen lima beans
Chopped fresh parsley
Assorted Toppings (suggestions follow)

Combine pork hocks, water, tomatoes, onion, garlic, salt and chili powder in 8-qt. kettle. Cover and cook over high heat until mixture comes to a boil; reduce heat to low. Simmer 1½ hours, or until pork is tender.

Remove pork hocks. Discard fat and bones. Cut up meat and return to broth.

Skim off fat from broth. Add corn and lima beans. Cook over high heat until mixture comes to a boil; reduce heat to low. Simmer, uncovered, 15 minutes, or until beans are tender.

Ladle soup into bowls and garnish with parsley. Pass several bowls of the Assorted Toppings to spoon on soup. Makes about 4 quarts.

Assorted Toppings: Shredded carrots, chopped lettuce, sliced radishes, sliced green onions, avocado cubes and shredded Monterey Jack or Muenster cheese.

Hearty Bean Soup

4 strips bacon
1 c. cubed fully cooked ham
½ c. chopped onion
½ c. chopped green pepper
2 (16-oz.) cans tomatoes, cut up
1 c. water
2 tblsp. brown sugar, packed
2 tblsp. vinegar
1 tsp. salt
2 (22-oz.) jars New England-style baked beans

Fry bacon in 4-qt. Dutch oven or saucepan over medium heat until browned. Remove bacon and drain on paper towels. Pour off all but 2 tblsp. bacon drippings. Crumble bacon; set aside.

Cook ham, onion and green pepper in bacon drippings until meat is browned and vegetables are tender. Add tomatoes, water, brown sugar, vinegar and salt. Cook over high heat until mixture comes to a boil; reduce heat to low. Cover and simmer 10 minutes.

Reserve 2 c. beans. Mash the remaining beans. Add whole and mashed beans to soup. Stir in bacon. Heat thoroughly, stirring occasionally. Makes about 2 quarts.

Split Pea Soup

1 lb. dry green split peas
2 qt. water
1 lb. ham hocks or 1 meaty ham bone
1½ c. chopped onion
2 tsp. salt
¼ tsp. pepper
¼ tsp. dried marjoram leaves
1 c. chopped celery
1 c. cubed pared potatoes
1 c. sliced pared carrots

Wash and sort peas. Combine peas, water, ham hocks, onion, salt, pepper and marjoram in 4-qt. Dutch oven. Cook over high heat until mixture comes to a boil; reduce heat to low. Cover and simmer 1½ hours, stirring occasionally.

Remove ham. Discard fat and bones. Cut meat into pieces and return to soup mixture. Add celery, potatoes and carrots. Cover and simmer over low heat 30 minutes, stirring occasionally, or until vegetables are tender. Makes about 2 quarts.

Lentil Sausage Soup

 1 lb. fresh pork sausage links
 3 tblsp. water
 2 c. chopped onion
 1 clove garlic, minced
 2½ qt. water
 2 c. dried lentils, rinsed and drained
 1 (16-oz.) can tomatoes, cut up
 4 carrots, pared and sliced
 ¾ c. sliced celery
 ¼ c. chopped fresh parsley
 1½ tblsp. salt
 ½ tsp. dried marjoram leaves
 ¼ tsp. pepper

Place sausage and 3 tblsp. water in 4-qt. Dutch oven. Cover and cook over medium heat 5 minutes. Remove cover; continue cooking until sausage is browned, turning frequently. Remove sausage and drain on paper towels. Cut into chunks; set aside.

Pour off all but ¼ c. pan drippings. Sauté onion and garlic in drippings over medium heat until tender. Add remaining ingredients. Cook over high heat until mixture comes to a boil; reduce heat to low. Cover and simmer 25 to 30 minutes, or until vegetables are tender.

Add sausage chunks and heat thoroughly. Makes 3 quarts.

Pasta and Bean Soup

> 1 lb. dry Great Northern beans
> 2 qt. water
> 2½ tsp. salt
> 1 large carrot, pared
> 6 strips bacon
> ½ c. chopped onion
> ½ c. chopped celery
> 1 small clove garlic, minced
> 1 (16-oz.) can stewed tomatoes
> ¼ c. water
> ½ bay leaf
> ½ tsp. dried oregano leaves
> ½ tsp. salt
> ¼ tsp. pepper
> 1 c. ditalini or small elbow macaroni,
>   cooked and drained

Soak beans in 6-qt. Dutch oven with enough water to cover, 8 hours or overnight.

Rinse and drain. Combine beans, 2 qt. water, 2½ tsp. salt and carrot in 6-qt. Dutch oven. Cook over high heat until mixture comes to a boil; reduce heat to low. Cover and simmer 2 hours, or until beans are tender.

Fry bacon in 10″ skillet over medium heat until browned. Remove and drain on paper towels. Crumble and set aside.

Pour off all but ¼ c. bacon drippings. Add onion, celery and garlic to bacon drippings in skillet. Sauté over medium heat until tender. Stir in stewed tomatoes, ¼ c. water, bay leaf, oregano, ½ tsp. salt and pepper. Cook over high heat until mixture comes to a boil; reduce heat to low. Simmer, uncovered, 30 minutes.

Remove half of the beans. Purée beans in blender until smooth. Pour puréed beans back into Dutch oven. Remove carrot and cut up. Add chopped carrot, cooked macaroni and bacon to Dutch oven. Heat thoroughly. Makes 3½ quarts.

September Cheese Soup

½ c. butter or regular margarine
1⅓ c. finely chopped pared carrots
1 c. chopped celery
½ c. chopped onion
2 (13¾-oz.) cans chicken broth
⅔ c. flour
½ tsp. salt
¼ tsp. pepper
1 qt. milk
2 c. shredded Cheddar cheese (8 oz.)

Melt butter in 4-qt. Dutch oven over medium heat, about 2 minutes. Add carrots, celery and onion and sauté until tender. Add chicken broth. Cook over high heat until mixture comes to a boil; reduce heat to low. Cover and simmer 10 minutes.

Combine flour, salt and pepper in bowl and gradually blend in milk. Add milk mixture to chicken broth mixture in Dutch oven and cook over medium heat, stirring constantly, until mixture boils and thickens. Add Cheddar cheese; cook and stir just until cheese is melted. Makes about 2 quarts.

Barbecued Beef Buns

1½ lb. ground beef
1 c. chopped onion
1½ c. ketchup
1 c. water
¼ c. sugar
¼ c. Worcestershire sauce
2 tblsp. vinegar
2 tblsp. lemon juice
4 tsp. prepared yellow mustard
2 tsp. salt
¼ tsp. pepper
⅛ tsp. cayenne pepper
12 hamburger buns, split

Cook ground beef in 12" skillet over medium heat until meat turns color. Add onion and cook until meat is well browned. Drain off excess fat.

Add ketchup, water, sugar, Worcestershire sauce, vinegar, lemon juice, mustard, salt, pepper and cayenne pepper. Cook until mixture comes to a boil; reduce heat to low. Simmer, uncovered, 30 minutes, stirring occasionally.

Spoon meat mixture into hamburger buns. Makes 12 servings.

Open-Face Burgers

1 lb. ground beef
1 (16-oz.) can tomatoes, cut up
2 tsp. instant minced onion
1 tsp. salt
1 tsp. chili powder
½ tsp. cornstarch
½ tsp. ground cumin
½ tsp. crushed dried red pepper
½ tsp. instant minced garlic
¼ tsp. dried oregano leaves
6 hamburger buns, split and toasted
2 c. finely shredded lettuce
1½ c. shredded Cheddar cheese (6 oz.)
½ c. finely chopped onion

Brown ground beef in 10″ skillet over medium heat; drain off excess fat. Stir in tomatoes, instant onion, salt, chili powder, cornstarch, cumin, red pepper, instant garlic and oregano. Cook over medium heat until mixture comes to a boil; reduce heat to low. Simmer, uncovered, 10 minutes.

Spoon meat mixture over bun halves and sprinkle with lettuce, Cheddar cheese and onion. Makes 6 servings.

Monterey Spoonburgers

1 lb. ground beef
¾ c. chopped onion
¾ c. chopped celery
¾ c. bottled barbecue sauce
¾ c. ketchup
¼ tsp. salt
8 hamburger buns, split and toasted

Cook ground beef with onion and celery in 10″ skillet over medium heat until meat is browned. Drain off excess fat.

Add barbecue sauce, ketchup and salt. Cook until mixture comes to a boil; reduce heat to low. Cover and simmer 20 minutes, stirring occasionally.

Spoon meat mixture into buns. Makes 8 servings.

Pizza Burgers

½ lb. ground beef
½ lb. bulk pork sausage
½ c. ketchup
⅓ c. water
1 tsp. dried oregano leaves
¼ tsp. salt
¼ c. dry bread crumbs
6 hamburger buns, split
3 slices American cheese

Brown ground beef and sausage in 10″ skillet over medium heat. Drain off excess fat. Stir in ketchup, water, oregano, salt and bread crumbs. Heat meat mixture thoroughly.

Lay opened hamburger buns on broiler pan. Spoon meat mixture on bottoms of hamburger buns. Cut each slice of American cheese into 4 strips. Lay 2 strips of cheese crisscross fashion over meat mixture on each bun.

Place under broiler just until cheese melts. Makes 6 servings.

Beef Stroganoff Sandwiches

1 (1-lb.) loaf French bread
1 lb. ground beef
¼ c. finely chopped onion
1 c. dairy sour cream
¼ c. chopped fresh parsley
1 tblsp. milk
1 tsp. salt
⅛ tsp. pepper
1 tsp. Worcestershire sauce
1½ c. shredded process American cheese (6 oz.)

Cut French bread in half lengthwise. Wrap in foil and heat in 375° oven 10 minutes.

Meanwhile, cook ground beef and onion in 10″ skillet over medium heat until meat is browned. Drain off excess fat. Stir in sour cream, parsley, milk, salt, pepper and Worcestershire sauce. Heat thoroughly, but do not boil.

Spread meat mixture over cut surface of both halves of bread. Sprinkle with American cheese. Place on baking sheet and return to oven; bake 5 minutes, or until cheese is melted. Cut each piece into four slices. Makes 8 servings.

Pizza Loaf

> **1 (1-lb.) loaf French bread, or 4 long Italian rolls**
> **3 tblsp. butter or regular margarine**
> **¾ lb. ground beef**
> **½ c. grated Parmesan cheese**
> **1½ tsp. minced onion**
> **1½ (6-oz.) cans tomato paste**
> **¼ c. sliced pimiento-stuffed olives**
> **½ tsp. dried oregano leaves**
> **1 tsp. salt**
> **⅛ tsp. pepper**
> **2 medium tomatoes, thinly sliced**
> **8 slices process American cheese**

Cut French bread loaf or Italian rolls in half lengthwise. Spread with butter.

Combine ground beef, Parmesan cheese, onion, tomato paste, olives, oregano, salt and pepper in bowl; mix lightly, but well. Spread mixture on cut sides of bread loaf or rolls.

Place bread halves, meat side up, on baking sheet. Top with tomato slices.

Bake in 350° oven 20 minutes. Remove from oven; top with American cheese slices. Return to oven and bake 5 minutes more, or until cheese is melted. Cut each piece, if using French bread, into four slices. Makes 8 servings.

Runzas

2 (13¾-oz.) pkg. hot roll mix
1 lb. ground beef
1 lb. bulk pork sausage
3 c. chopped cabbage
2 c. finely chopped onion
1 c. shredded pared carrots
2 tblsp. water
1 tblsp. Worcestershire sauce
1½ tsp. salt
½ tsp. dried oregano leaves
½ tsp. ground nutmeg
¼ tsp. pepper
1 egg, beaten
1 tblsp. water

Prepare hot roll mix according to package directions and let rise until doubled.

Meanwhile, brown ground beef and pork sausage in 12" skillet over medium heat. Drain off excess fat.

Combine cabbage, onion, carrots and 2 tblsp. water in 10" skillet. Cover and steam over medium heat 10 minutes.

Drain vegetable mixture. Add to browned meat with Worcestershire sauce, salt, oregano, nutmeg and pepper. Cool completely.

Turn dough onto floured surface. Divide dough into 12 parts. Roll each into a 6" circle. Place ½ c. meat mixture in center of each circle. Bring edges of circle to center and pinch together. Place, 3 inches apart, on greased baking sheets. Brush with combined egg and 1 tblsp. water. Let rise in warm place 30 minutes.

Bake in 400° oven 15 minutes, or until golden brown. Serve warm or cold. Makes 12 servings.

Grilled Reuben Sandwiches

1 (16-oz.) can sauerkraut, rinsed and drained
½ c. bottled Russian salad dressing
6 slices boiled ham
6 slices Swiss cheese
6 slices cooked chicken or turkey
12 slices pumpernickel bread
4 tblsp. butter or regular margarine

Combine sauerkraut with Russian dressing in bowl. Place
1 slice each of ham, Swiss cheese and chicken on each of 6 slices
of bread. Top each with sauerkraut mixture, then another slice of
bread. Butter top side of sandwiches, using about 1 tsp. butter on
each.

Heat 12″ skillet over medium heat, about 5 minutes. Place
3 sandwiches at a time in hot skillet, buttered side down. Butter
top side of sandwiches. Cook sandwiches about 3 minutes on
each side, or until both sides are browned and cheese is melted.

Repeat with remaining sandwiches. Makes 6 servings.

French Ham Sandwiches

12 slices bread
6 slices boiled ham or chopped luncheon meat
6 slices process American cheese
6 thin slices tomato
2 eggs, slightly beaten
½ c. milk
1½ c. crushed potato chips
3 tblsp. butter or regular margarine

Top each of 6 slices of bread with 1 slice each of ham, American cheese and tomato. Top each with another slice of bread.

Blend together eggs and milk in pie plate. Dip sandwiches in egg-milk mixture coating both sides well. Be sure to use all of egg-milk mixture. Then dip both sides of sandwiches in potato chips.

Melt butter in 12″ skillet over medium heat, about 2 minutes. Cook 3 sandwiches at a time, about 4 minutes on each side, or until both sides are browned and cheese is melted.

Repeat with remaining sandwiches. Makes 6 servings.

Turkey-Cheese Sandwiches

Easy Thousand Island Dressing (recipe follows)
12 strips bacon
12 slices rye bread, buttered
8 oz. slices cooked turkey
8 oz. Swiss cheese, thinly sliced
6 c. shredded lettuce
12 tomato wedges

Prepare Easy Thousand Island Dressing
Cut bacon in half crosswise; fry in 10″ skillet over medium heat until browned. Drain on paper towels; set aside.
On each of 6 plates place 2 slices buttered bread, side by side. Make open-face sandwiches as follows: Cover bread slices with turkey and Swiss cheese. Mound 1 c. lettuce over cheese; spoon ½ c. Easy Thousand Island Dressing over each serving. Top each with 4 half slices cooked bacon. Garnish each serving with tomato wedges. Makes 6 servings.

Easy Thousand Island Dressing: Combine 2⅓ c. mayonnaise or salad dressing, 2 chopped hard-cooked eggs, ⅓ c. chili sauce, 3 tblsp. chopped dill pickle and 2 tsp. grated onion in bowl. Cover and chill in refrigerator several hours to blend flavors. Makes 3 cups.

Tuna Club Sandwiches

2 cucumbers, pared and thinly sliced
Salt
2 tblsp. vinegar
2 tblsp. salad oil
1/8 tsp. pepper
1/8 tsp. dried dill weed
2 (7-oz.) cans tuna, drained and flaked
1 c. chopped celery
1/2 c. chopped fresh parsley
1/2 c. mayonnaise or salad dressing
18 slices bread, toasted
4 tblsp. butter or regular margarine
6 hard-cooked eggs, sliced

Sprinkle cucumbers with salt in bowl. Let stand 1 hour. Place cucumbers in strainer; rinse with cold water and drain. Place drained cucumbers in bowl. Stir in vinegar, oil, pepper and dill weed. Marinate at least 30 minutes. Drain.

Combine tuna, celery, parsley and mayonnaise in bowl. Mix until well blended.

Spread 6 slices of toast with butter. Spread each with 1/2 c. tuna mixture. Top each with a slice of toast, then with egg slices and drained cucumber slices.

Butter remaining 6 slices of toast; place buttered side down over cucumber slices. Cut sandwiches diagonally in halves. Hold layers of each sandwich half together with wood picks. Makes 6 servings.

Hot Tuna Buns

1 (7-oz.) can tuna, drained and flaked
3 hard-cooked eggs, chopped
4 oz. process American cheese, cubed
2 tblsp. pickle relish
2 tblsp. finely chopped onion
1 tblsp. finely chopped green pepper
½ c. mayonnaise or salad dressing
6 hamburger buns, split

Combine tuna, eggs, American cheese, pickle relish, onion, green pepper and mayonnaise in bowl. Mix well. Fill buns with tuna mixture. Place in 13x9x2" baking pan; cover tightly with aluminum foil.

Bake in 375° oven 20 minutes, or until cheese is melted. Makes 6 servings.

Open-Face Bean Sandwiches

6 slices bread, toasted
1 (22-oz.) jar New England-style baked beans,
 drained
6 tblsp. ketchup
3 onion slices, separated into rings
12 strips bacon, partially cooked

Top each slice of toast with about ⅓ c. baked beans, then with 1 tblsp. ketchup and a few onion rings. Place sandwiches on broiler pan. Broil 4″ from source of heat about 2 minutes, or until ketchup bubbles.

Top each sandwich with 2 slices bacon. Continue broiling 1 to 2 minutes, or until bacon is cooked. Makes 6 servings.

Hot Dog Curls

1 tblsp. butter or regular margarine
½ c. chopped onion
½ c. chopped green pepper
½ c. chopped celery
1 lb. frankfurters, sliced lengthwise
1 tblsp. flour
1 (8-oz.) can tomato sauce
½ c. water
6 frankfurter buns, split and toasted

Melt butter in 10″ skillet over medium heat, about 2 minutes. Add onion, green pepper and celery and sauté until tender.

Add frankfurters and fry until they curl up and are deep red in color. Stir in flour and cook until lightly browned. Stir in tomato sauce and water. Reduce heat to low. Cover and simmer 10 minutes.

Spoon frankfurter mixture into buns. Makes 6 servings.

Macaroni-Cheese Bake

¼ c. butter or regular margarine
2 c. sliced onion
3 (16-oz.) cans stewed tomatoes
1½ tsp. Worcestershire sauce
1 tsp. salt
¼ tsp. pepper
12 oz. elbow macaroni, cooked and drained
2 c. shredded Cheddar cheese (8 oz.)

Melt butter in 12″ skillet over medium heat, about 2 minutes. Add onion and sauté until tender.

Add stewed tomatoes, Worcestershire sauce, salt and pepper. Cook over high heat until it comes to a boil; reduce heat to low. Simmer, uncovered, 5 minutes.

Combine tomato mixture with macaroni; mix well. Alternate layers of macaroni mixture and Cheddar cheese in greased 3-qt. casserole, ending with layer of cheese.

Bake in 375° oven 30 minutes, or until hot and bubbly. Makes 6 to 8 servings.

Quick Chili Beans

1 (15-oz.) can chili without beans
1 (16-oz.) can barbecue-style beans
1 (5½-oz.) bag tortilla chips
¾ c. chopped onion
2 c. shredded Longhorn cheese (8 oz.)

Combine chili and barbecue-style beans in bowl. Set aside.
Crumble one third of the tortilla chips in bottom of greased
1½-qt. glass loaf dish. Spoon one half of the chili-bean mixture
over chips. Sprinkle with one half of the onion and one half of
the Longhorn cheese. Top with one third of the crumbled tortilla
chips. Repeat layers, ending with tortilla chips. .

Bake in 350° oven 30 minutes, or until hot and bubbly. Makes
4 servings.

Curried Creamed Eggs

12 strips bacon
3 tblsp. butter or regular margarine
1/4 c. finely chopped onion
1/4 c. finely chopped celery
1/4 c. finely chopped green pepper
5 tblsp. flour
1 tsp. curry powder
1/16 tsp. pepper
1 (13 3/4-oz.) can chicken broth
1 1/4 c. milk
6 hard-cooked eggs, sliced
9 slices bread, toasted and cut in half
   diagonally

Fry bacon in 12" skillet over medium heat until browned. Remove bacon; drain on paper towels.

Pour off all but 3 tblsp. bacon drippings. Add butter to bacon drippings in skillet. Heat over medium heat until butter is melted. Add onion, celery and green pepper. Sauté 8 minutes, or until tender.

Stir flour, curry powder and pepper into skillet. Cook, stirring constantly, 1 minute. Gradually stir chicken broth and milk into flour mixture. Cook, stirring constantly, until mixture boils and thickens, about 7 minutes. Cook 1 minute more. Stir in hard-cooked eggs. Cook 2 minutes more, or until eggs are hot.

For each serving, arrange 3 toasted bread halves on plate. Place 2 strips bacon on toast. Spoon 2/3 c. egg mixture over all. Makes 6 servings.

Crustless Bacon Quiche

8 strips bacon, diced
3 eggs
1½ c. milk
½ c. buttermilk baking mix
½ c. butter or regular margarine, melted
Dash of pepper
1 c. shredded Cheddar cheese (4 oz.)

Fry bacon in 10″ skillet over medium heat until browned. Remove bacon with slotted spoon; drain on paper towels.

Combine eggs, milk, baking mix, melted butter and pepper in blender. Cover and blend 15 seconds, or until well mixed.

Pour mixture into greased 9″ glass pie plate. Sprinkle with bacon and Cheddar cheese. Gently press bacon and cheese below surface, using the back of a spoon.

Bake in 350° oven 30 minutes, or until knife inserted halfway between center and edge comes out clean. Let stand 10 minutes before serving. Makes 6 servings.

Chapter Three

Side Dishes from the Garden

Vegetables and salads add variety, color, texture and flavor to everyday meals. And, as a special bonus, they contribute vitamins to your family's diet.

In this collection of 11 vegetable favorites, we've included a simple Herbed Asparagus—fresh asparagus spears seasoned with lemon juice and basil. Another choice, Skillet Cabbage, is a great end-of-the-season combination: cabbage, green pepper, onion and tomatoes quickly cooked in a skillet. Potato fans will love Low-Calorie Potato Scallop flavored with lots of thinly sliced onions and chicken broth and dusted with paprika.

Timesaving vegetable combinations, such as Freeze-Ahead Orange Carrots or Freeze-Ahead Potato Puffs, are easy on the cook and help turn an ordinary meal into an event.

You'll also discover 10 different salads from basic crisp greens to festive molds. Our Overnight Green Salad is far from ordinary though—it's made a day in advance and "frosted"

with mayonnaise-sour cream dressing. If your family likes coleslaw, try our make-ahead Tangy Coleslaw—its flavor improves with overnight chilling.

Tasty, economical potato salads are easy to prepare and equally successful at picnics or indoor dinners. Sour Cream Potato Salad features sliced new potatoes marinated in Italian dressing before being mixed with cucumbers, green onions, hard-cooked eggs and a sour cream-mayonnaise dressing.

Since molded salads can be prepared in advance and always make a hit with everyone, we include several. Our Molded Spring Salad features lime gelatin and cottage cheese along with radishes, peas and green pepper. If you like fruit salads, try Jellied Waldorf Salad brimming with raisins, apples, celery and walnuts.

When a vegetable hater reaches for seconds or a child asks for a salad again, you'll know your extra time was rewarded in planning these special menu go-withs.

Herbed Asparagus

4 lb. fresh asparagus
3 tsp. salt
¼ c. butter or regular margarine
2 tblsp. lemon juice
½ tsp. dried basil leaves

Scrub asparagus thoroughly to remove sand. Remove tough ends.

Spread stalks in 4-qt. Dutch oven or 12" skillet. Sprinkle with salt. Add 2" boiling water. Place over high heat and boil, uncovered, 5 minutes. Cover and cook 7 to 10 minutes longer, or until stalks are tender-crisp. Drain well.

Melt butter in small saucepan over medium heat. Stir in lemon juice and basil. Pour over asparagus. Makes 8 servings.

Lima Beans au Gratin

1 lb. dried large lima beans, cooked
¼ c. butter or regular margarine
¼ c. chopped onion
¼ c. chopped celery
¼ c. flour
1 c. milk
1 c. evaporated milk
1½ c. shredded Cheddar cheese (6 oz.)
3 tblsp. diced pimiento
½ tsp. salt
¼ tsp. dried thyme leaves
Paprika

Drain lima beans, reserving ¼ c. cooking liquid.

Melt butter in 2-qt. saucepan over medium heat. Add onion and celery and sauté until tender. Stir in flour; cook, stirring constantly, 1 minute. Gradually stir in milk, evaporated milk and reserved cooking liquid. Cook until mixture thickens and boils, stirring constantly.

Stir in 1 c. of the Cheddar cheese; continue stirring until cheese is melted. Add pimiento, salt and thyme. Remove from heat.

Place beans and sauce in alternate layers in greased 2-qt. casserole, ending with sauce. Top with remaining ½ c. Cheddar cheese. Sprinkle with paprika.

Bake in 350° oven 1 hour, or until golden brown. Makes 6 servings.

Skillet Cabbage

2 tblsp. cooking oil
3 c. coarsely chopped cabbage
2 c. chopped seeded tomatoes
1 c. chopped celery
¾ c. chopped green pepper
½ c. chopped onion
1 tsp. sugar
¾ tsp. salt
¼ tsp. pepper

Heat oil in 10″ skillet over medium heat. Add remaining ingredients; mix well.

Cover and cook over medium heat 10 minutes, or until cabbage is tender-crisp. Makes 6 servings.

Butternut Squash with Peas

2 (1-lb.) butternut squash
½ tsp. salt
1 (10-oz.) pkg. frozen peas
3 tblsp. butter or regular margarine

Pare squash. Cut in half and remove seeds. Cut into 1″ chunks.

Heat 1″ water and salt in 3-qt. saucepan over high heat until it comes to a boil. Add squash and return to a boil. Reduce heat to low. Cover and simmer 10 minutes.

Add peas. Cook, covered, 5 to 7 minutes more, or until vegetables are tender. Drain well. Add butter and toss gently. Makes 6 servings.

Freeze-Ahead Orange Carrots

1½ lb. carrots, pared and cut into 2x¼" strips
¼ c. brown sugar, packed
2 tsp. flour
½ tsp. salt
½ c. orange juice
1 tblsp. lemon juice
1 tblsp. vinegar
1 tblsp. grated orange rind
2 tblsp. butter or regular margarine

Blanch carrots in boiling water in 4-qt. Dutch oven 5 minutes. Drain. Place carrots in aluminum foil-lined 8" square glass baking dish. Set aside.

Blend together brown sugar, flour and salt in small saucepan. Add orange juice, lemon juice, vinegar and orange rind. Cook over medium heat until mixture comes to a boil, stirring constantly. Add butter and cook, uncovered, 5 minutes more.

Pour sauce over carrots in dish and freeze. Remove from dish; wrap and store in freezer up to 6 weeks.

To serve, unwrap carrots and place upside down in same dish. Cover with foil and bake in 350° oven 40 minutes. Uncover and bake 20 minutes, or until carrots are tender. Makes 6 servings.

Potatoes and Peas au Gratin

**1 (10¾-oz.) can condensed cream of mushroom
  soup
1 c. milk
1 c. shredded sharp Cheddar cheese (4 oz.)
5 c. sliced pared Idaho potatoes (¼" thick),
  cooked and drained
½ c. cooked peas
1 tblsp. chopped pimiento**

Combine cream of mushroom soup, milk and Cheddar cheese
in 2-qt. saucepan. Cook over medium heat, stirring, until cheese
melts. Remove from heat. Combine potatoes, peas, pimiento and
soup mixture in bowl; toss gently to mix. Arrange in 8" square
glass baking dish. Cover with aluminum foil.

Bake in 400° oven 25 minutes. Remove foil; bake 10 minutes
more, or until hot and bubbly. Makes 6 servings.

Golden Potato Squares

½ lb. bacon, diced
2 c. diced pared Idaho potatoes
2 c. milk
1 (5-oz.) jar process cheese spread with bacon
1 tsp. instant minced onion
2 eggs, beaten
1 tblsp. minced fresh parsley
½ tsp. dry mustard
½ tsp. salt
1/16 tsp. pepper

Fry bacon in 10" skillet over medium heat until browned. Remove with slotted spoon and drain on paper towels. Set aside.

Place potatoes in 1" water in 2-qt. saucepan. Cover and cook over high heat until it comes to a boil. Remove from heat; drain in colander. Arrange potatoes in 8" square glass baking dish.

Combine milk, cheese spread and onion in 2-qt. saucepan. Cook over medium heat, stirring constantly, until cheese melts. Combine eggs, parsley, mustard, salt and pepper in bowl. Slowly stir hot cheese mixture into egg mixture. Pour over potatoes.

Bake in 325° oven 30 minutes. Top with bacon. Bake 5 minutes more, or until knife inserted in center comes out clean. Remove from oven; let stand 5 minutes before serving. Makes 9 servings.

Low-Calorie Potato Scallop

> 2 lb. all-purpose potatoes, pared and thinly
>   sliced (about 5 c.)
> 1 c. thinly sliced onion
> 2 tblsp. flour
> 1 tsp. salt
> 1/8 tsp. pepper
> 1 c. skim milk, scalded
> 1 c. chicken broth
> Paprika

Arrange one third of the potatoes in lightly greased 2-qt. casserole. Arrange one third of the onion on top of the potatoes. Combine flour, salt and pepper. Sprinkle one third of flour mixture over potatoes and onion. Repeat layers twice. Pour hot milk and chicken broth over all. Sprinkle with paprika. Cover with lid or aluminum foil.

Bake in 375° oven 1 hour 15 minutes. Uncover and bake 30 minutes more, or until potatoes are tender. Makes 6 to 8 servings.

Freeze-Ahead Potato Puffs

4 strips bacon, diced
Mashed Potatoes (recipe follows)
2 tblsp. minced fresh parsley
¼ c. flour
¼ tsp. salt
2 eggs, slightly beaten
1 c. fine dry bread crumbs
½ c. cooking oil

Fry bacon in 10″ skillet over medium heat until browned. Remove with slotted spoon and drain on paper towels.

Prepare Mashed Potatoes.

Add bacon and parsley to Mashed Potatoes; mix well. Shape into 40 (1¾″) logs, using 1½ tblsp. potato mixture for each.

Combine flour and salt. Roll potato puffs in flour mixture; then dip in eggs. Roll in bread crumbs. Place on baking sheet. Freeze 2½ hours, or until firm. Wrap in aluminum foil. Freeze up to 4 weeks.

To cook, pour oil into 12″ electric frypan; heat to 340°. Add half of the frozen potato puffs to the hot oil. Fry, turning frequently, 8 minutes, or until golden. Remove puffs; drain on paper towels. Repeat with remaining potato puffs. Makes 8 servings.

Mashed Potatoes: Cook 8 medium (2½ lb.) all-purpose potatoes (pared and quartered) with 1 tsp. salt in boiling water in 4-qt. Dutch oven 20 minutes, or until tender. Drain. Mash potatoes with vegetable masher until smooth. Stir in ⅓ c. milk, ½ tsp. salt and 1/16 tsp. pepper. Cool at room temperature, about 45 minutes before shaping.

Rice Ring with Vegetables

5 c. water
2 tblsp. butter or regular margarine
2 tsp. salt
2½ c. uncooked regular rice
3 tblsp. minced fresh parsley
1 tblsp. minced onion
Cheese Egg Sauce (recipe follows)
4 c. hot cooked mixed vegetables

Bring water, butter and salt to a boil in 3-qt. saucepan over high heat. Slowly stir in rice. Cook until mixture returns to a boil; reduce heat to low. Cover and cook 15 minutes, or until water is absorbed. Remove from heat. Stir in parsley and onion.

Meanwhile, prepare Cheese Egg Sauce.

Spoon hot rice mixture into 6-c. ring mold. (Do not pack.) Turn out immediately on serving plate. Fill center of ring with cooked vegetables. Spoon ½ c. of Cheese Egg Sauce over rice ring. Pass remaining sauce in small bowl. Makes 8 servings.

Cheese Egg Sauce: Melt 4 tblsp. butter or regular margarine in 3-qt. saucepan over medium heat. Stir in 4 tblsp. flour and ½ tsp. salt. Cook over medium heat, stirring constantly, 1 minute. Gradually stir in 3 c. milk. Cook, stirring constantly, until mixture boils and thickens. Stir in 1 c. shredded Cheddar cheese (4 oz.).

Add some of the hot cheese mixture to 2 well-beaten eggs. Mix well. Stir egg mixture back into hot cheese mixture. Cook over low heat 1 minute, stirring constantly. Makes 4 c. sauce.

Sweet-and-Sour Baked Beans

½ c. cooking oil or bacon drippings
1 c. chopped onion
1 clove garlic, minced
1 (15-oz.) can tomato sauce
1 c. chopped celery
½ c. chili sauce
¼ c. dark brown sugar, packed
¼ c. dark molasses
1 tsp. salt
¼ tsp. pepper
2 dashes Tabasco sauce
1 lb. dried navy beans, cooked and drained
1 (13½-oz.) can pineapple chunks, drained and
   cut in half
½ c. chopped sweet pickles
¼ c. sliced stuffed olives

Heat cooking oil or bacon drippings in 4-qt. Dutch oven over medium heat, about 2 minutes. Sauté onion and garlic in hot oil until tender. Stir in tomato sauce, celery, chili sauce, brown sugar, molasses, salt, pepper and Tabasco sauce. Cook until mixture comes to a boil; reduce heat to low. Simmer, uncovered, 20 minutes.

Add cooked navy beans, pineapple, pickles and olives; mix well. Turn into 3-qt. casserole; cover with lid or aluminum foil.

Bake in 350° oven 1 hour. Uncover; bake 15 minutes more, or until hot and bubbly. Makes 8 to 10 servings.

Overnight Green Salad

1 lb. bacon, diced
1 medium head iceberg lettuce
1 (10-oz.) pkg. fresh spinach
1 pt. cherry tomatoes, halved
1 (10-oz.) pkg. frozen peas, thawed
1/2 c. sliced green onions
1 1/2 c. mayonnaise
1 c. dairy sour cream
2 tblsp. lemon juice
1/2 tsp. dried oregano leaves
1/4 tsp. dried basil leaves
1/4 tsp. salt
1/8 tsp. pepper

Fry bacon in 10″ skillet over medium heat until browned. Remove with slotted spoon and drain on paper towels. Set aside.

Tear lettuce and spinach into bite-size pieces and place in a very large salad bowl. Add cherry tomatoes, peas, bacon and green onions; toss gently.

Combine mayonnaise, sour cream, lemon juice, oregano, basil, salt and pepper in bowl; mix well. Spread dressing over greens; be sure to "frost" entire surface. (Do not mix in.) Cover with plastic wrap. Refrigerate salad mixture overnight.

Just before serving, toss dressing with greens. Makes 8 servings.

Wilted Spinach Salad

6 c. fresh spinach, torn into bite-size pieces
3 hard-cooked eggs, coarsely chopped
¼ c. sliced green onions
5 strips bacon, diced
¼ c. vinegar
2 tblsp. water
2 tblsp. sugar
¼ tsp. salt
¼ tsp. pepper

Combine spinach, eggs and green onions in salad bowl.
Cook bacon in 10″ skillet over medium heat until browned.
Remove bacon with slotted spoon and drain on paper towels.
Pour off all but 3 tblsp. bacon drippings.

Add vinegar, water, sugar, salt and pepper to bacon drippings.
Cook until mixture comes to a boil over medium heat, stirring to
blend. Pour over spinach mixture; toss gently. Sprinkle with
bacon. Makes 6 servings.

Tangy Coleslaw

1 c. cider vinegar
1 c. sugar
¾ tsp. mustard seed
¾ tsp. celery seed
½ tsp. salt
¼ tsp. ground turmeric
10 c. shredded cabbage
1½ c. chopped onion
1 (4-oz.) jar pimientos, drained and chopped

Combine vinegar, sugar, mustard seed, celery seed, salt and turmeric in 2-qt. saucepan. Cook over medium heat, stirring occasionally, until mixture boils. Remove from heat and cool to room temperature.

Combine cabbage, onion and pimientos in large bowl. Pour vinegar mixture over cabbage mixture, tossing to coat. Cover and chill in refrigerator overnight. Makes 12 servings.

Kidney Bean Salad

5 (15-oz.) cans red kidney beans, drained
1 c. chopped onion
½ c. chopped celery
⅓ c. sweet pickle relish
½ c. cider vinegar
½ c. sugar
1 egg, slightly beaten
2 tsp. dry mustard

Combine kidney beans, onion, celery and pickle relish in bowl; set aside.

Combine vinegar, sugar, egg and mustard in small saucepan. Cook over low heat 7 minutes, stirring constantly, or until mixture thickens. (Do not boil.)

Pour vinegar mixture over vegetables, tossing gently to coat. Cover and chill in refrigerator at least 6 hours. Makes 16 servings.

Sour Cream Potato Salad

2½ lb. new potatoes
½ tsp. salt
½ c. bottled Italian salad dressing
4 hard-cooked eggs
¾ c. thinly sliced celery
⅔ c. sliced green onions
1½ c. mayonnaise
½ c. dairy sour cream
1½ tsp. prepared yellow mustard
¾ tsp. salt
½ tsp. prepared horseradish
¼ tsp. celery seed
⅛ tsp. pepper
⅔ c. chopped pared cucumber
1 tblsp. sliced green onion tops

Cook potatoes in 1" boiling water with ½ tsp. salt in 4-qt. Dutch oven 30 minutes, or until tender. Drain; cool 10 minutes. Peel potatoes and slice into bowl. Pour Italian dressing over potatoes. Cover; refrigerate 2 hours.

Remove yolks from eggs; set aside. Chop egg whites. Toss egg whites, celery and green onions with potatoes. Press egg yolks through sieve. Reserve 2 tblsp. sieved egg yolk. Mix together remaining egg yolks, mayonnaise, sour cream, mustard, ¾ tsp. salt, horseradish, celery seed and pepper in bowl. Pour mayonnaise mixture over potatoes. Toss lightly. Cover and refrigerate at least 2 hours.

Before serving, toss cucumbers with potato salad. Garnish with reserved sieved egg yolk and green onion tops. Makes 2 quarts or 16 servings.

Molded Potato Salad

1 (8-oz.) jar gherkin pickles
Water
1 env. unflavored gelatin
10 small pimiento-stuffed olives, sliced
1½ c. mayonnaise or salad dressing
2 tsp. salt
¼ tsp. Tabasco sauce
5 c. diced pared new potatoes, cooked and
    drained
½ c. chopped celery
¼ c. minced onion
3 hard-cooked eggs, diced

Drain pickles, reserving juice. Add enough water to juice to make 1 c. Chop enough pickles to make ¼ c.; set aside.

Sprinkle gelatin over pickle juice in small saucepan. Cook over low heat, stirring constantly, until gelatin dissolves. Remove from heat. Reserve ⅓ c.; let remaining gelatin stand at room temperature.

Pour half of reserved ⅓ c. gelatin in bottom of lightly oiled 2-qt. ring mold. Arrange olives in gelatin. Chill in refrigerator until set. Pour remaining part of ⅓ c. gelatin on top. Chill in refrigerator until set.

Combine remaining gelatin, mayonnaise, salt and Tabasco sauce in bowl. Beat with rotary beater until smooth.

Combine potatoes, celery, onion, eggs and ¼ c. chopped pickles in bowl. Pour mayonnaise mixture over potato mixture. Toss lightly until well mixed. Pour mixture into prepared mold. Cover and chill in refrigerator until set. Makes 8 servings.

Fruit and Rice Salad

2 c. cooked regular rice
1 (20-oz.) can crushed pineapple, drained
2 c. miniature marshmallows
½ c. sugar
3 medium unpared apples, cored and cubed
½ c. sliced red maraschino cherries
1 c. heavy cream, whipped

Combine cooked rice, pineapple, marshmallows and sugar in bowl; toss gently to mix. Cover and refrigerate at least 3 hours.

Fold in apples and cherries. Then fold in whipped cream. Cover and chill 1 hour more. Makes 18 servings.

Garden-Fresh Vegetable Mold

1 (3-oz.) pkg. lemon flavor gelatin
½ tsp. salt
1 c. boiling water
¾ c. cold water
1 tblsp. vinegar
¾ c. peeled, seeded and diced tomato
¾ c. grated pared carrot
3 tblsp. minced green onions
2 tblsp. finely chopped green pepper

Dissolve lemon flavor gelatin and salt in boiling water in bowl. Stir in cold water and vinegar. Chill in refrigerator until thick and syrupy.

Fold in tomato, carrot, green onions and green pepper. Pour gelatin mixture into lightly oiled 4-c. mold. Cover and chill in refrigerator until set. Makes 4 to 6 servings.

Molded Spring Salad

1 (3-oz.) pkg. lime flavor gelatin
1 c. boiling water
1 c. mayonnaise or salad dressing
1 c. creamed small curd cottage cheese
¹/₈ tsp. salt
1 c. cooked peas
¹/₂ c. chopped radishes
¹/₂ c. chopped green pepper
1 tblsp. minced onion

Dissolve lime flavor gelatin in boiling water in bowl. Beat in mayonnaise until smooth, using a rotary beater. Stir in cottage cheese and salt. Chill in refrigerator until thick and syrupy.

Fold in peas, radishes, green pepper and onion. Pour gelatin mixture into a lightly oiled 5-c. mold. Cover and chill in refrigerator until set. Makes 6 servings.

Jellied Waldorf Salad

> **2 (3-oz.) pkg. lemon flavor gelatin**
> **1½ c. boiling water**
> **1½ c. cold water**
> **¼ c. golden raisins**
> **Boiling water**
> **1 c. diced unpared red apple**
> **½ c. diced celery**
> **¼ c. chopped walnuts**

Dissolve lemon flavor gelatin in 1½ c. boiling water in bowl. Stir in cold water. Chill in refrigerator until thick and syrupy.

Meanwhile, cover raisins with boiling water. Let stand 10 minutes. Drain; set aside.

Fold apple, celery, walnuts and raisins into gelatin. Pour into lightly oiled 5-c. mold. Cover and chill in refrigerator until set. Makes 6 to 8 servings.

Chapter Four

Country-Style Desserts

When you plan dessert, select a sweet that complements the rest of the meal. A heavily spiced or sauced entrée calls for a light, refreshing dessert, whereas a light main dish leaves room for richer finales. Each dessert in this chapter is quick and easy, but still has all the flavor you'd expect in an old-fashioned dessert.

Both cake lovers and cooks will like our good, basic cakes—they are all easily prepared from scratch and don't need frosting. Airy Sponge Cake Squares are drizzled with lots of melted butter and sprinkled with cinnamon and confectioners' sugar before serving. If your family likes chocolate, our Chocolate Fudge Cake is perfect. It's made with chocolate-flavored syrup— no fuss with melting chocolate. Home-style Spicy Applesauce Cake is flavored just right with cinnamon and cloves and filled with raisins and pecans. These cakes are all good alone or alongside ice cream, pudding or fresh fruit.

Of course, you'll find other dependable desserts, such as Cranberry-Apple Crisp combining tart red cranberries with sweet apple slices topped with a brown sugar-oat mixture. We give a choice of two pudding cakes: Lemon or Chocolate Pudding Cake. While baking, each one separates into a tender cake layer with smooth, creamy pudding sauce underneath. These oven desserts are best served slightly warm with a spoon of ice cream or whipped cream.

There's always pie, and we've chosen two of the best: Creamy Custard Pie, delicately set with a touch of nutmeg, and Mock Pecan Pie, containing nutlike cereal instead of the more expensive pecans. If you freeze a few pie shells ahead when you have a little time, you can mix these up in a jiffy.

If you're looking for something special or expecting guests, present Layered Strawberry Delight, a spring treat layered with buttercream filling, sliced strawberries, whipped cream and a scattering of chopped pecans.

Whether you serve these desserts as part of a meal or between meals with coffee, we're sure they'll highlight the moment.

Chocolate Fudge Cake

1 c. sifted flour
1 tsp. baking powder
½ c. butter or regular margarine
1 c. sugar
4 eggs
1 tsp. vanilla
1 (16-oz.) can chocolate-flavored syrup
1 c. chopped walnuts
Confectioners' sugar

Sift together flour and baking powder; set aside.

Cream together butter and sugar in bowl until light and fluffy, using electric mixer at medium speed. Add eggs, one at a time, beating well after each addition. Beat in vanilla.

Add dry ingredients alternately with chocolate-flavored syrup to creamed mixture, beating well after each addition, using electric mixer at low speed. Stir in walnuts. Pour batter into greased and floured 9" tube pan.

Bake in 350° oven 1 hour 5 minutes, or until cake tester or wooden pick inserted in center comes out clean. Cool in pan on rack 15 minutes. Remove from pan; cool completely on rack.

Sprinkle cake with confectioners' sugar before serving. Makes 12 servings.

Banana Streusel Cake

1 c. sifted flour
1½ tsp. baking powder
½ tsp. baking soda
½ tsp. salt
½ tsp. ground cinnamon
¾ c. sifted flour
½ c. sugar
½ c. butter or regular margarine
¼ c. sugar
2 eggs
1 tsp. vanilla
⅔ c. mashed bananas
⅓ c. buttermilk

Sift together 1 c. flour, baking powder, baking soda, salt and cinnamon; set aside.

Combine ¾ c. flour and ½ c. sugar in bowl. Cut in butter until mixture is crumbly, using a pastry blender. Reserve ½ c. crumb mixture.

Add ¼ c. sugar, eggs and vanilla to remaining crumb mixture. Beat until smooth, using electric mixer at medium speed.

Add dry ingredients alternately with combined bananas and buttermilk to egg mixture, beating well after each addition, using electric mixer at low speed. Spread batter in greased 10″ pie plate. Sprinkle with reserved ½ c. crumb mixture.

Bake in 375° oven 35 minutes, or until cake tester or wooden pick inserted in center comes out clean. Cool on rack. Serve in wedges. Makes 8 servings.

Spicy Applesauce Cake

1½ c. sifted flour
1 tsp. baking soda
1 tsp. salt
1 tsp. ground cinnamon
¼ tsp. ground cloves
½ c. shortening
1 c. sugar
2 eggs
1 c. applesauce
1 c. raisins
1 c. chopped pecans
1 tblsp. flour

Sift together 1½ c. flour, baking soda, salt, cinnamon and cloves; set aside.

Cream together shortening and sugar in bowl until light and fluffy, using electric mixer at medium speed. Add eggs, one at a time, beating well after each addition.

Add dry ingredients alternately with applesauce to creamed mixture, beating well after each addition, using electric mixer at low speed. Combine raisins, pecans and 1 tblsp. flour. Stir into batter. Pour batter into greased 9″ square baking pan.

Bake in 350° oven 55 minutes, or until cake tester or wooden pick inserted in center comes out clean. Cool in pan on rack. Cut into squares. Makes 9 servings.

Blueberry Surprise Cake

2 c. sifted flour
1 c. sugar
2 tsp. baking powder
½ tsp. salt
½ c. butter or regular margarine
2 eggs
½ c. milk
1 tsp. vanilla
1 (24-oz.) jar blueberry pie filling
¼ c. sugar

Sift together flour, 1 c. sugar, baking powder and salt into bowl. Cut in butter until mixture is crumbly, using a pastry blender. Reserve ½ c. crumb mixture.

Beat together eggs, milk and vanilla in another bowl. Add to remaining crumb mixture; stir well. Spread batter in greased 13x9x2" pan.

Combine blueberry pie filling and ¼ c. sugar in bowl. Spread over top of batter. Sprinkle with reserved ½ c. crumb mixture.

Bake in 325° oven 45 minutes, or until cake tester or wooden pick inserted in center comes out clean. Cool in pan on rack. Makes 16 servings.

Sponge Cake Squares

1½ c. sifted flour
1½ tsp. baking powder
¼ tsp. salt
3 eggs
1½ c. sugar
1 tsp. vanilla
¾ c. milk, scalded
½ c. butter or regular margarine, melted
Confectioners' sugar
Ground cinnamon

Sift together flour, baking powder and salt; set aside.

Beat eggs in bowl, using electric mixer at high speed. Gradually beat in sugar; continue beating until thick and light. Add vanilla. Beat in hot milk.

Gradually beat in dry ingredients, using electric mixer at low speed. Pour batter into greased and floured 13x9x2" baking pan.

Bake in 350° oven 40 minutes, or until top springs back when touched lightly with finger. Remove cake from oven. Slowly pour melted butter over top. Sprinkle with confectioners' sugar, then cinnamon. Cool in pan on rack. Makes 12 servings.

Brownie Pudding Cake

1½ c. sifted flour
1 c. sugar
3 tblsp. baking cocoa
3 tsp. baking powder
¾ tsp. salt
¾ c. milk
1½ tblsp. butter or regular margarine, melted
2 tsp. vanilla
¾ c. chopped walnuts
5 drops red food coloring
½ c. brown sugar, packed
¼ c. sugar
3 tblsp. baking cocoa
1¾ c. boiling water

Sift together flour, 1 c. sugar, 3 tblsp. cocoa, baking powder and salt into bowl. Add milk, butter and vanilla; beat well, using a spoon. Stir in walnuts and food coloring. Spread batter in greased 13x9x2″ baking pan.

Combine brown sugar, ¼ c. sugar and 3 tblsp. cocoa in bowl; mix well. Sprinkle over batter. Pour boiling water overall.

Bake in 350° oven 40 minutes, or until top springs back when touched lightly with finger. Makes 12 servings.

Lemon Pudding Cake

1½ c. sugar
½ c. sifted flour
½ tsp. salt
4 eggs, separated
⅓ c. lemon juice
1 tsp. grated lemon rind
1 tblsp. butter or regular margarine, melted
1½ c. milk
Sweetened whipped cream

Sift together sugar, flour and salt; set aside.

Beat together egg yolks, lemon juice, lemon rind and butter in bowl until thick and lemon-colored, using electric mixer at high speed.

Add dry ingredients alternately with milk to egg mixture, beating well after each addition, using electric mixer at low speed.

Beat egg whites in bowl until stiff (but not dry) peaks form, using electric mixer at high speed. Blend egg whites into batter, using electric mixer at low speed. Pour into 8″ square glass baking dish. Set dish in pan and fill with hot water to a depth of 1″.

Bake in 350° oven 45 minutes, or until golden brown. Serve warm topped with whipped cream. Makes 8 servings.

Caramel Bread Pudding

> 2 tblsp. butter or regular margarine
> 1 c. brown sugar, packed
> 6 slices white bread, cut into ½ ″ cubes
> 6 eggs
> ½ c. brown sugar, packed
> 2 c. milk
> 1 tsp. vanilla
> ⅛ tsp. salt

Generously coat the inside of double boiler top with butter. Place 1 c. brown sugar into buttered double boiler top and sprinkle with bread cubes. (Do not mix.)

Beat eggs well in bowl, using rotary beater. Gradually beat in ½ c. brown sugar, milk, vanilla and salt. Pour over bread cubes. (Do not stir.) Place over simmering water. Cover and cook 1 hour 30 minutes. Serve warm. Makes 6 to 8 servings.

Orange County Rice Pudding

3 c. reconstituted nonfat dry milk
½ c. uncooked regular rice
½ c. sugar
¼ tsp. salt
½ tsp. grated orange rind
½ tsp. grated lemon rind
1 tsp. vanilla
¾ c. creamed small curd cottage cheese

Scald milk in top of double boiler over simmering water. Stir in rice, sugar and salt. Cover and cook 30 to 40 minutes, or until thickened and rice is tender.

Remove from heat and add orange rind, lemon rind and vanilla. Cover and chill in refrigerator.

Beat cottage cheese with spoon until smooth. Fold into chilled pudding mixture. Makes 6 servings.

Orange Snow Pudding

1 env. unflavored gelatin
¼ c. cold water
1 c. sugar
¾ c. boiling water
½ c. orange juice
3 egg whites
1½ tsp. grated orange rind
Custard Sauce (recipe follows)

Soften gelatin in cold water in bowl 5 minutes. Add sugar and boiling water, stirring until gelatin and sugar dissolve. Stir in orange juice. Chill in refrigerator until almost set, about 1½ hours.

Beat egg whites in large bowl, using electric mixer at high speed, until stiff (but not dry) peaks form. Beat gelatin mixture until foamy, using electric mixer at high speed. Fold gelatin mixture and orange rind into egg whites. Cover and chill in refrigerator until set, about 3 hours. Meanwhile, prepare Custard Sauce (recipe follows).

To serve, spoon pudding into sherbet glasses and top with Custard Sauce. Makes 6 servings.

Custard Sauce: Combine 3 egg yolks, 2 tblsp. sugar and dash of salt in top of double boiler. Gradually stir in 1 c. milk (scalded). Place over hot (not boiling) water. Cook, stirring constantly, until mixture coats a metal spoon. Stir in ½ tsp. vanilla. Pour into metal bowl. Cover and chill in refrigerator.

Dessert Dumplings

Dessert Sauce (recipes follow)
2/3 c. sifted flour
2 tblsp. sugar
3/4 tsp. baking powder
1/8 tsp. salt
1 tblsp. butter or regular margarine
1 egg, beaten
1 tblsp. milk
1/4 tsp. vanilla

Prepare one of the dessert sauces below.

Sift together flour, sugar, baking powder and salt into bowl. Cut in butter until mixture is crumbly, using a pastry blender. Add egg, milk and vanilla; mix just until moistened.

Bring prepared Dessert Sauce to a boil over medium heat. Drop dumpling mixture by spoonfuls into boiling sauce, making 8 dumplings. Reduce heat to low; cover and cook 20 minutes. (Do not remove cover during cooking period.) Makes 4 servings.

Maraschino Cherry Sauce: Drain 1 (8-oz.) jar maraschino cherries, reserving 1/2 c. juice. Chop cherries; set aside. Combine 1/2 c. sugar, 3 tblsp. cornstarch and 1/4 tsp. salt in 10" skillet. Gradually stir in 1/2 c. cherry juice and 1 1/2 c. water. Add cherries, 1/4 c. butter or regular margarine, 1 tblsp. lemon juice, 1/2 tsp. almond extract, 1/2 tsp. grated lemon rind and 3 drops red food coloring. Cook over medium heat until mixture comes to a boil, stirring constantly. Reduce heat to low. Simmer 1 minute. Set aside; prepare Dumplings.

Orange Sauce: Combine 1/4 c. sugar, 4 tsp. cornstarch and dash of salt in 10" skillet. Stir in 1 1/4 c. reconstituted frozen orange juice, 1/2 c. water, 1 tblsp. butter or regular margarine and 1/2 tsp. grated orange rind. Cook over medium heat until mixture comes to a boil, stirring constantly. Reduce heat to low. Simmer 2 minutes. Set aside; prepare Dumplings.

Cranberry-Apple Crisp

3 c. sliced pared apples
2 c. fresh or frozen cranberries
1 c. sugar
1 tblsp. lemon juice
¼ tsp. salt
1 c. brown sugar, packed
1 c. quick-cooking oats
½ c. unsifted flour
⅓ c. butter or regular margarine
Vanilla ice cream

Combine apples, cranberries, sugar, lemon juice and salt in bowl. Toss lightly to mix. Turn fruit mixture into greased 8" square glass baking dish.

Combine brown sugar, oats and flour in bowl. Cut in butter until mixture is crumbly, using a pastry blender. Sprinkle over fruit mixture in dish.

Bake in 325° oven 50 minutes, or until fruit is tender and top is golden brown. Cool on rack 45 minutes. Serve warm topped with vanilla ice cream. Makes 6 servings.

Grandmom's Apricot Squares

1½ c. sifted flour
1½ c. quick-cooking oats
1 c. brown sugar, packed
¾ c. butter or regular margarine
1 (10-oz.) jar apricot preserves (1 c.)

Mix together flour, oats and brown sugar in bowl. Cut in butter until mixture is crumbly, using a pastry blender. Press two thirds of crumb mixture into greased 8" square baking pan, building up sides to make a ½" rim.

Spread apricot preserves over crumb layer. Sprinkle remaining crumb mixture on top; pat down gently.

Bake in 350° oven 35 minutes, or until golden brown. Cool in pan on rack. When completely cooled, cut into 2" squares. Makes 16 servings.

Chewy Fudge Brownies

¼ c. butter or regular margarine
3 (1-oz.) squares unsweetened chocolate
1⅓ c. sugar
2 eggs
½ c. unsifted self-rising flour
1 tsp. vanilla
⅔ c. chopped pecans

Combine butter and chocolate in small saucepan. Melt over low heat. Remove from heat. Pour chocolate mixture into bowl. Add sugar and eggs. Beat until well blended, using electric mixer at medium speed. Stir in flour and vanilla. Then stir in pecans. Spread mixture in greased 9″ square baking pan.

Bake in 325° oven 30 minutes, or until cake tester or wooden pick inserted in center comes out clean. Cool in pan on rack. While still warm, cut into 2″ squares. Makes 16.

Mock Pecan Pie

¾ c. crunchy nutlike cereal nuggets
½ c. warm water
3 eggs
¾ c. sugar
1 c. dark corn syrup
3 tblsp. butter or regular margarine, melted
1 tsp. vanilla
⅛ tsp. salt
1 unbaked 9″ pie shell

Combine cereal and warm water in bowl. Let stand until water is absorbed.

Combine eggs and sugar in another bowl. Beat until well blended, using electric mixer at medium speed. Beat in corn syrup, butter, vanilla and salt; blend well. Stir in cereal mixture. Pour mixture into pie shell.

Bake in 350° oven 50 minutes, or until top of pie is puffy and golden brown. Cool on rack. Makes 6 to 8 servings.

Creamy Custard Pie

4 eggs, slightly beaten
½ c. sugar
¼ tsp. salt
3 c. milk, scalded
1 tsp. vanilla
1 unbaked 9″ pie shell
Ground nutmeg

Beat together eggs, sugar and salt in bowl, using a rotary beater. Slowly beat in milk and vanilla. Pour custard mixture into pie shell. Sprinkle top with nutmeg.

Bake in 450° oven 10 minutes. Reduce heat to 325° and bake 30 to 40 minutes, or until knife inserted halfway between center and edge of pie comes out clean. Cool on rack. Refrigerate if stored overnight. Makes 6 to 8 servings.

Lemon-Lime Supreme

1 (3-oz.) pkg. lime flavor gelatin
¼ tsp. salt
3 eggs, separated
⅓ c. lime juice
¼ c. lemon juice
⅓ c. water
¼ tsp. cream of tartar
⅓ c. sugar
1 c. heavy cream, whipped

Combine lime flavor gelatin, salt, egg yolks, lime juice, lemon juice and water in small saucepan; mix well. Cook over medium heat, stirring constantly, until mixture comes to a boil. Remove from heat; pour into a bowl. Chill in refrigerator until thick and syrupy.

Beat egg whites in bowl until foamy, using electric mixer at high speed. Add cream of tartar. Gradually add sugar, beating until stiff glossy peaks form. Fold egg whites and whipped cream into gelatin mixture. Pour into 1½-qt. serving bowl. Cover and chill in refrigerator until set. Makes 6 to 8 servings.

Lemon Delight

1 env. unflavored gelatin
½ c. cold water
3 eggs, separated
½ c. sugar
½ tsp. salt
½ tsp. grated lemon rind
½ c. lemon juice
1 c. marshmallow creme
¼ c. sugar
1 (2-oz.) env. whipped topping mix
½ c. milk
1 tsp. vanilla
⅓ c. chopped walnuts

Soften gelatin in cold water in bowl 5 minutes. Combine egg yolks, ½ c. sugar, salt, lemon rind and lemon juice in top of double boiler; mix well. Cook over simmering water 7 minutes, stirring constantly, or until mixture thickens. Remove from heat.

Stir in softened gelatin. Add marshmallow creme, stirring until melted. Chill in refrigerator until thick and syrupy.

Beat egg whites in bowl until foamy, using electric mixer at high speed. Gradually add ¼ c. sugar, beating until soft peaks form. Fold egg white mixture into chilled lemon mixture. Pour into lightly oiled 8" square glass baking dish. Cover and chill in refrigerator until set.

Prepare whipped topping mix with milk and vanilla according to package directions. Cover and chill in refrigerator until serving time.

Cut dessert into squares. Top each with prepared whipped topping and walnuts. Makes 9 servings.

Fruited Dessert Squares

> 1 (3-oz.) pkg. cherry flavor gelatin
> 1 c. boiling water
> 1⅓ c. graham cracker crumbs
> 3 tblsp. sugar
> ⅓ c. butter or regular margarine, melted
> 12 red maraschino cherries, chopped
> 3 bananas, diced
> 2 c. heavy cream, whipped

Dissolve cherry flavor gelatin in boiling water in bowl. Chill in refrigerator until thick and syrupy.

Meanwhile, combine graham cracker crumbs, sugar and butter in bowl; mix well. Press mixture in bottom and up sides of 9" square baking pan.

Fold maraschino cherries and bananas into thickened gelatin. Then fold in whipped cream. Pour mixture into graham cracker crust. Cover and chill in refrigerator until set. Cut into squares. Makes 9 servings.

Layered Strawberry Delight

1 c. graham cracker crumbs
1 c. butter or regular margarine
3⅓ c. sifted confectioners' sugar
3 eggs
1 tsp. vanilla
4 c. sliced fresh strawberries
2 c. heavy cream
¼ c. sugar
1 tsp. vanilla
⅓ c. chopped pecans

Spread graham cracker crumbs in bottom of 13x9x2" (3-qt.) glass baking dish.

Cream together butter and 3 c. of the confectioners' sugar in bowl until light and fluffy, using electric mixer at medium speed. Add eggs; beat well. Blend in 1 tsp. vanilla. Drop mixture by spoonfuls over crumbs; spread carefully with spatula.

Combine strawberries with remaining ⅓ c. confectioners' sugar in bowl. Arrange on creamed layer. Refrigerate.

Whip cream until it begins to thicken, using electric mixer at medium-high speed. Gradually beat in sugar and 1 tsp. vanilla. Beat until soft peaks form. Spread whipped cream over strawberries. Sprinkle with pecans. Cover and chill in refrigerator 2 hours.

Cut into squares. Makes 16 servings.

Note: Dessert can be frozen ahead. To serve, let thaw in refrigerator 8 hours or overnight.

Crunchy Ice Cream Squares

1 c. brown sugar, packed
½ c. butter or regular margarine
2½ c. coarsely crushed cornflakes
½ c. chopped Spanish peanuts
½ c. flaked coconut
1 qt. vanilla ice cream, softened

Combine brown sugar and butter in small saucepan. Cook over medium heat until butter melts and sugar is dissolved. Combine with cornflakes, peanuts and coconut in bowl.

Press one half of mixture in greased 12x8x2" (2-qt.) glass baking dish. Spread with softened ice cream. Top with remaining crumb mixture. Cover and freeze until firm. Cut into squares. Makes 8 servings.

Index

Index

Index

Index

Index

Index